Cromwell's Head

Cromwell's Head

JONATHAN FITZGIBBONS

*

the national archives

First published in 2008 by
The National Archives
Kew, Richmond
Surrey TW9 4DU
United Kingdom

www.nationalarchives.gov.uk

The National Archives brings together the Public Record Office,
Historical Manuscripts Commission, Office of Public Sector Information
and Her Majesty's Stationery Office.

A catalogue card for this book is available from the British Library.

ISBN 978 1 905615 38 4

Jacket, typographic design and typesetting by
Ken Wilson | point918

Printed in Great Britain by
Biddles Ltd, King's Lynn

COVER ILLUSTRATION
Detail from a portrait of Oliver Cromwell
after Robert Walker, *c.*1649,
Bridgeman Art Library.

Contents

Introduction

ON THE AFTERNOON of Friday 3 September 1658, London was subjected to some of the heaviest winds in living memory. As the hurricane raging outside battered houses and tore down trees, the atmosphere inside the palace of Whitehall was equally stormy. Lying on his deathbed, Oliver Cromwell, Lord Protector of England, Scotland and Ireland, was drawing his final breath. Hitherto, this had been renowned as his 'lucky day', the date on which he had decimated the Scots at Dunbar in 1650, and decisively subdued the forces of Charles II at Worcester in 1651. Seven years on, he was now locked in one final battle with death itself. It was a fight that, for once, the great Parliamentarian general could not win. Sometime before four o'clock in the afternoon, Oliver passed away, aged 59.

This outcome, if generally feared, was not totally un-expected. Since the death of his 'favourite' daughter Elizabeth from cancer on 6 August 1658, Cromwell had been a broken man. Just days later he fell into his fatal illness. On 17 August, Cromwell's son-in-law Charles Fleetwood informed Oliver's fourth son and Lord Deputy of Ireland, Henry Cromwell, that since Elizabeth's death, 'his Highnes hath bine very much indisposed, troubled with paynes in his bowells & backe & could not sleepe'.[1] That same day, the Quaker leader George Fox rode to Hampton Court to try to have a word with the Lord Protector. Although Fox found Cromwell riding in the palace park, the mortal disease that gripped him was all too apparent: 'I saw and felt a waft of death go forth against him; and when I came to him he looked a dead man'.[2] By 21 August, Cromwell's distemper had manifested itself as 'a tertian ague'; a form of malaria that was surprisingly common in Western Europe at the time. With violent fits recurring every other day, on 24 August—'this being the interval day'—Cromwell moved from Hampton Court to Whitehall, in the hope that the 'change of aire' would aid his recovery.[3]

It did not. On 30 August, Secretary of State John Thurloe calculated that this was now the '13th day since his ague took him'. To make matters worse, 'upon saterday' 28 August it had fallen into 'a double tertian, haveinge 2 fitts in 24 houres, one upon the heeles of another'.[4] For most of his final days Cromwell was in constant fits. Dr Thomas Clarges pertinently summed up the situation on 1 September: 'His disease is a double tertian ague, which at this season, in a person of his age and constitution of body (being much distemper'd by his late grief and melancholly, besides his other infirmities) is a very violent companion.'[5] It would be romantic to suggest that Oliver Cromwell died from a broken heart following the death of his daughter. Yet, the most probable immediate cause seems to have been septicemia contracted through a urinary infection brought on by his weakened feverish state.

* * *

The impact of Cromwell's death on those around him was profound. A mixture of blind panic and ecstatic eulogizing consumed Whitehall. Leading the tributes to his former master, in a particularly cringeworthy letter to Henry Cromwell, was Secretary Thurloe:

> I am not able to speake or write; this stroake is soe soare, soe unexpected, the providence of God in it soe stupendious, consideringe the person that is fallen, the tyme and season wherein God tooke hym away, with other circumstances, I can doe nothinge but put my mouthe in the dust, and say, it is the Lord; and though his wayes be not alwayes knowne, yet they are alwayes righteous, and wee must submitt to his will … he is gone to heaven, embalmed with the teares of his people, and upon the winges of the prayers of the saints.[6]

At a loss to explain why Cromwell was taken in his prime, this devastating blow was written off as the mysterious workings of God. Cromwell's illness and death was a warning to the nation as a whole to repent its sins. According to Fleetwood 'it is for sin, we are thus rebuked'. In order to redress this divine punishment, he hoped that 'the Lord give us hearts to know every one the evill of our hearts & wayes that we may turn at his reproofe'.[7]

Toadying tributes filled the official newspaper reports of Oliver's death. The most striking compared the achievements of Lord Protector Cromwell with those of his monarchical predecessors, albeit Oliver outdid them all:

> His Wisdom and Piety in things divine, his Prudence in management of Civil Affairs, made him a Prince indeed among the people of God ... Thus it hath proved to him to be a day of Triumph indeed, there being much of Providence in it, that after so glorious Crowns of Victory [i.e. Dunbar and Worcester] placed on his head by God on this day, having neglected an Earthly Crown, he should now go to receive the Crown of Everlasting Life.[8]

Having famously refused the Crown in life, Cromwell now received a heavenly crown in death. Two months later, this rhetorical device would take new meaning as the Lord Protector's funeral displayed all the trappings of a pompous, monarchical pageant.

Indeed, the most striking thing about the funeral of Cromwell was that it was distinctly 'un-Cromwellian'. From the beginning, the funeral had been planned as a

truly regal affair. On 24 September, the Venetian resident
Francesco Giavarina reported that, 'it was decided to follow the forms observed at the burial of King James'.[9]
Four days later, Henry Cromwell was informed that his
father's funeral solemnities, 'will bee much after the
manner of the late king James's'.[10] The government's newspapers announced how Cromwell's body was to lie at
Somerset House, 'as becomes the dignity and renown of
so great a Prince'. It was to be 'after the ancient and most
becoming Ceremony of the preceding Princes of this
Nation upon the like occasion'.[11]

On 20 September the funeral ceremonials began with
the removal of Cromwell's body from Whitehall to
Somerset House to lie in state. The location was perhaps
no coincidence; it was the same royal residence where
James I had lain in state over 30 years earlier. Preparations
were quite protracted and some time passed before the
coffin went on display. When Somerset House was finally
opened to the public on 18 October, the full extent of the
lavish arrangements was revealed. No expense was spared
on the sumptuous decoration in the various mourning
chambers, hung with velvet and adorned with shields bearing the Protectoral coat of arms 'crowned with the Imperial Crown' (see plate 3). The body itself was not visible,
but lay sealed in its coffin within an elaborately constructed 'Bed of State'. Instead, lying on top of the coffin,
symbolically taking the place of the dead Protector, was
a lifelike effigy. With the face modelled in wax from

Cromwell's death mask (see plate 4), the likeness was truly remarkable. Yet, even more incredible was the effigy's apparel. According to newspaper reports it was dressed:

> in a rich Suit of uncut Velvet, being robed first in a Kirtle Robe of Purple Velvet, laced with a rich gold lace, and furr'd wih Ermins; upon the Kirtle is the Royal large Robe of the like Purple Velvet laced, and fur'd with Ermins, with rich strings, and tassels of gold; his Kirtle is girt with a rich Embroidered Belt, in which is a fair Sword richly gilt, and hatcht with gold hanging by the side of the Effigies; in the right hand is the golden Scepter representing Government; in his left hand is held the Globe, representing Principality; upon his head, the Cap of Regality of Purple Velvet, furr'd with Ermins. Behind the head is a rich chair of Estate of cloth of gold tissued; upon the Cushion of the Chair stands the Imperial Crown set with stones.[12]

Clearly those making the arrangements for the funeral had followed royal precedent down to the smallest detail.

Somerset House was bustling with spectators meandering through the various rooms leading to the hearse. Despite the throng of people, the mood was sombre. As the crowds passed along bareheaded and in 'solemn silence', the former gentlemen of Cromwell's household ushered them on—giving them only a brief glimpse of the effigy. As one witness wrote, 'when you come into the Room where the Effigies was and the bed of state, you were not to be permitted to continue any time'. Instead, he explained, the spectators had to quickly 'passe along into another Room where the Back Stairs were, to represent unto us how transitory this life is, and the Glory of this world'.[13]

The monarchical nature of the show stepped up another notch on 12 November when Cromwell's effigy was moved into a standing position. The strange spectacle led one observer to joke how 'the old Protector is now got upon his legs again in Somerset house' as if resurrected from the dead.[14] This 'standing in state' had actually been a traditional part of royal funerals. It was an enduring remnant of the Catholic faith, marking the soul's passage from purgatory into Heaven. Thus the effigy was 'placed standing upon an Ascent, under a rich Cloth of Estate, being vested with Royal Robes, a Scepter in one hand, a Globe in the other, and a Crown on the head'.[15] The eyes on the effigy were now opened and gazed out eerily towards the onlookers. Compared to the darkened rooms of the lying-in-state, this new display was lit by 'four or five hundred candles set in flat shining candlesticks' that 'were so placed round near the roof of the hall, that the light they gave seemed like the rays of the sun'.[16] This was the most remarkable instance yet of Oliver Cromwell taking on the mantle of a king.

The most extravagant part of the ceremonials, however, was undoubtedly the funeral procession, which had been delayed twice, partly through faltering preparations, but finally took place on 23 November 1658. Ironically, Cromwell's body had been interred at Westminster Abbey two weeks earlier because of its advancing state of decomposition—by that point he had been dead for over two months—and therefore played no part in the funeral.

This minor detail did not keep the crowds away. Thousands of spectators from as far away as Cornwall and Orkney turned out to line the processional route from Somerset House to Westminster Abbey. According to one eyewitness, Abraham Cowley, it was 'the vast multitude of spectators' that made up 'no small part of the spectacle it self'.[17] The Quaker Edward Burrough was passing through the capital on the day of the funeral, when he arrived at Charing Cross and came across:

a very great multitude of people gathering together, and thronging, and pressing exceedingly, and the whole streets were filled from one side to another, upwards and downwards, so far as I could see, with abundance gazing forth at every Window, and upon the Balconies, and house tops, and the glass was pulled down for people to look out into the streets, and an exceeding number of people there was, all the streets so thronged, that I thought it could not be possible that any more could throng in, or pass by.[18]

The atmosphere was electric. Everybody stood waiting for a view of the lengthy procession as it snaked its way to the abbey.

On sheer weight of numbers, the funeral procession was extremely impressive. It included all the men of the Protectoral household, from household kitchen servants to the Lord Chamberlain Sir Gilbert Pickering. There were clerks, military officers, physicians, chaplains, judges, privy councillors, foreign ambassadors and numerous relatives of the Lord Protector. A banner or standard headed each 'section' of the funeral. According to the council's lavish instructions, 'To every standard must be a Horse covered with black cloth, adorned & garnished with Plumes, Shafferons & Escutcheons of the same Standard. Every Horse led by two Querries & a Groome to attend … attended also with Fife, Drumes and Trumpetts'.[19] The drums boomed, the trumpets sounded and banners and ribbons fluttered in the breeze as the procession passed by. For the waiting crowds, this was merely the preamble to the main spectacle of the day—the funeral chariot. Preceded by heralds, garbed in the Protector's coat of arms, this carriage was:

> adorned with Plumes and Escutcheons, and was drawn by six horses, covered with black Velvet, each of them likewise adorned with Plumes of Feathers … on each side of the Carriage were born the Banner-Roles being Twelve in number by Twelve persons of honor; and several pieces of his Highness Armor were born by honorable persons, Officers of the Army eight in number. After those noble persons who supported the Pall, followed Garter principal

King of Arms attended with a Gentleman on each side
bareheaded; next [i.e. after] him the chief Mourner; and
those Lords and noble persons that were Supporters, and
Assistants to the chief Mourner.[20]

Lying on top of the carriage was the effigy of Cromwell,
taken from Somerset House, still dressed in its regal robes
and wearing a crown upon its head.

On arrival at Westminster Abbey, 'the Hearse with the
Effigies thereon, was taken off the Carriage ... and in this
magnificent manner they carried it up to the East end of
the Abbey; and placed it in that Noble Structure which
was raised there on purpose to receive it; where it is to
remain for some time, exposed to publick view'. The
magnificent catafalque into which the hearse and effigy
were deposited was not unlike that erected for James I,
'but much more stately and expensive'. Cromwell was
clearly supposed to feel at home in this dormitory of
England's kings.

* * *

Yet Cromwell was *not* a king. He had refused to take the
title in his lifetime, and one cannot help but feel that this
pageant was constructing an image of Cromwell that he
himself would have found abhorrent. It is difficult to dis-
agree with the opinion of Edward Burrough, a man who
knew Cromwell and 'had the knowledge of his spirit',
when he claims:

I was perswaded if it had been asked him in his life time, if such work should be acted about him, such an Image made like him, and laid for so long a time in a sumptuous place and manner, and then carryed by his Friends, and Children, and Kindred, and Army; and then set up in such a place, and be removed from place to place; I say, I believe he would have denyed it, and said, It shall not be thus for me when I am dead.[21]

This pompous display was nothing more than 'foolery and foolishness, tending to the dishonour of a good man'. It was just as well that Oliver's body never took part in the vainglorious, idolatrous pageantry. Moreover, one must wonder what Cromwell would have made of the reported £60,000 expenditure (over £6.5 million in today's money) on his obsequies at a time when the government was severely in debt. Expensive, excessive and in no way reflecting the true nature of the man it sought to commemorate, George Wither was perhaps not alone in thinking the funeral 'a very costly Puppet-Play'.[22]

Cromwell's funeral was little more than a mirage; a crude manipulation of the Lord Protector's memory by certain persons within his government. Those responsible were the same people who had hoped to see him take the Crown in 1657 and now wished, with Cromwell dead, that the Protectorate would slide quickly and comfortably into a Cromwellian monarchy. Their reasons were clear enough; they disliked the destabilizing influence that the military had continued to exercise over Oliver's government. The funeral was a bid by the 'civilian' side of the Cromwellian privy council to imprint a particular image on the late Protector for their own ends: namely a more conservative, civilian-ized, respectable Cromwell that would appeal to the traditional elites of British society. Their ultimate aim was to make the Protectorate much more 'popular' among the traditional, conservative ruling classes and break free from military influence. Not for the last time, Cromwell's posthumous representation was being used for political ends.

Yet this veneer could not completely cover the cracks in the political fabric. The government was still beholden to the military interest, no matter how hard it tried to loosen the shackles. The funeral reaffirmed the Protectoral regime and the position of the army within it. On the day of the funeral, soldiers lined the streets of the processional route. Henry Fletcher later related how 'the Streets from Somerset-House to Westminster-Abby, were guarded by Souldiers in new Red Coats and black Buttons, with their Ensigns wrapt in Cypres'.[23] With pay in serious arrears and beginning to feel the winter's chill, the soldiers welcomed these coats provided by the new Protector—Cromwell's eldest surviving son, Richard— making the rank and file 'not a little joyfull in his favour'.[24] The whole route was also railed 'for the better conveniency of the passage'. On the day of the procession, 'no Coaches or Carts' could travel on the route from 'eight of the clock in the morning untill the solemnity was over that so neither the mourners in their Equipage, nor any other might be molested'.[25] Security was a pressing concern, and the army presence emphasized just how dependent the regime was on military strength.

Likewise, among the participants in the procession itself there was a noticeably high military presence. Besides the eight officers of the army who were armour bearers around the funeral chariot, a significant number of army officers also acted as banner and standard bearers. This had not been the intention of the council committee originally entrusted with the organization of the funeral. In mid-November it had ordered that:

> there be a perfect list made of all the mourners who are
> to proceed in the Funerall with their Qualities, Offices and
> dignities. That out of this list all persons of Honor and
> quality be appointed to be Assistants to the Chief Mourner,
> supporters to the Pall, to beare the Bannerolls, the great
> Banner, the Banners and Standards.[26]

The type of people they had in mind for these tasks was provided in a memorandum from the heralds. It was stated, for example, that the 'banner of Scotland' should be borne by 'two Scottish Earles'; the assistants to the Pall were to be 'six Earles'; the 'great Imbroidered Banner' to be carried by '2 Earles assisted with a Viscount'.[27]

These lofty plans failed to reflect political realities.

There simply were not enough 'earls' and 'viscounts' willing to turn out on behalf of the Cromwellian regime. Aspirations for a truly 'monarchical' funeral that would unite the traditional political elite behind the Protectorate clearly faltered. As a result, the civilians again found themselves dependent on the army. Of the 23 banner and standard bearers at Cromwell's funeral, all but two of them turned out to be men with military rank—none were earls or viscounts.[28] More significantly, the position of chief mourner would fall to the highest-ranking army officer, and Cromwell's son-in-law, Lieutenant-General Charles Fleetwood. Ironically, because Richard Cromwell followed 'royal' precedent and did not attend the funeral of his father, this had left the door open for the chief of the 'military' faction. Fleetwood, one of the men who had vehemently opposed Cromwell taking the Crown in his lifetime, now walked gravely behind an effigy of his former commander bedecked in all the ornaments of regality.

Thus the red coats, glistening armour and conspicuous presence of army officers around the hearse were all very visible signs that the military still had an important part to play in the Cromwellian government. What is more, the army felt obliged to be present at their commander's funeral. Cromwell was not just a head of state, he was a military hero who had fought, faced danger and achieved victory with them on the battlefields of the Civil Wars. As such, the army were keen to preserve another image of Cromwell that ran against the grain of the respectable, kingly representation of the civilians. Against the false image provided by the funeral effigy, the army's presence served to remind everyone of the true 'roots' of Cromwell's power. Like the personality and government of the person it sought to commemorate, Cromwell's funeral ended up being an ambivalent mix of both the military and the conservative.

*　*　*

To add to the government's woes, the solemnization of the funeral did not pass without incident. There had been some rumours of vandalism even before the funeral began. Edmund Ludlow noted how some, finding the pompous nature of the lying in state distasteful, 'threw dirt in the night' on the shield bearing the Cromwellian arms, which had been 'placed over the great gate of Somerset House'.[29] More violent was the claim by one Royalist that a group of 'Anabaptists' had got into Somerset House and there 'mett with what they saucely cald our Idol ... where they disgracefully tore of[f] his nose ... allso they lugged of[f] his eares, and cut of[f] his haire to his greate disfiguration'.[30] A number of hasty repairs had to be performed before the effigy could be ready for the procession. There was evidently a current of revulsion against official attempts to recast the late Lord Protector into King Oliver I.

When it came to the day of the funeral, John Evelyn,

no impartial observer, gives a flavour of the negative impact brought by the military contingent. While he points to the magnificence of the display, with 'Oliver lying in Effigie in royal robes, & Crown'd with a Crown, scepter & mound [i.e. globe] like a King', it was the irreverent presence of the soldiery that most caught Evelyn's attention. He confessed that 'it was the joyfullest funerall that ever I saw, for there was none that Cried, but dogs, which the souldiers hooted away with a barbarous noise; drinking, & taking Tobacco in the streetes as they went'.[31] This juxtaposition of the 'pomp' of the procession with the disorganized rabble of soldiers undermined the supposedly ordered and regal display.

The most significant disturbance to befall the pageantry, however, was very much self-inflicted. Although the procession was due to begin at eight in the morning, it was heavily delayed because of a dispute that arose between the foreign envoys and ambassadors over the issue of precedence. The French ambassador, Bordeaux, relates the mêlée that broke out on the morning of the funeral. The ambassadors 'had some dispute with the envoys of Sweden because they claimed to occupy the same rank as the rest'. The Swedish envoys argued that they had an equal right to march with the ambassadors and threatened to abstain from the funeral if that right was not recognized. Bordeaux immediately 'contested this equality' between envoys and ambassadors in the funeral procession, and in turn he too threatened to abstain. In the end, an expedient was worked out whereby 'the master of ceremonies and his officers took their places between them [the envoys] and us [the ambassadors]' to which Bordeaux grudgingly 'consented'.[32] The Venetian and Danish ambassadors were not so compromising, however, and withdrew in protest.

All this bickering cost time. The funeral procession took over seven hours to reach its destination, not arriving at Westminster Abbey until nightfall. When the effigy was taken into the abbey 'there was not a single candle … to give light to the company', and as a result, there were 'neither prayers, nor sermon, nor funeral oration, and after the trumpets had sounded for a short time, every one withdrew in no particular order'.[33] In many ways the funeral had proved a failure. Ridiculously expensive, overawed by the military and provoking a minor diplomatic incident, it did at least wow the crowds. Overall, it is hard to argue with Abraham Cowley's sneering summary of the day's events: 'Much noise, much tumult, much expence, much magnificence, much vain-glory; briefly, a great show, and yet after all this, but an ill sight.'[34]

* * *

Some three centuries later, on 25 March 1960, a very different ceremony took place at Oliver's old college: Sidney Sussex, Cambridge. Attended not by thousands, but by only seven people, it was a simple affair far removed from the street pageantry of November 1658. There were no trumpets, no ranks of mourners, no elaborate hearse, just a simple service conducted by the college chaplain. Yet this ceremony, unlike its predecessor, would actually see the final interment of Cromwell's remains. Buried in a casket not unlike a biscuit tin, in a secret location somewhere within the college, Oliver's head was given its inconspicuous interment. Unlike the magnificent monument once erected in Westminster Abbey, only a simple oval plaque in the college's antechapel marks this burial, merely stating: 'Near to this place was buried 25 March 1960 the head of Oliver Cromwell Lord Protector of the Commonwealth of England, Scotland & Ireland, Fellow Commoner of this College 1616–7' (see plate 23). That the location had to remain a secret indicates the emotions and curiosity that, even 300 years after his death, Cromwell could still excite. Only through a clandestine burial could Cromwell finally rest in peace.

Yet how did Cromwell's head come to be buried at Sidney Sussex? In the intervening period between the pomposity of the Lord Protector's funeral and the austere interment of his head, there is an intriguing story to be told. According to one account, on his deathbed Cromwell offered one final prayer: 'Pardon such as desire to trample upon the dust of a poor worm, for they are thy people too'.[35] Cromwell seemed to be offering forgiveness to those who sought to malign him in death; possibly even those who might literally 'trample upon' his 'dust'. His words were extremely prescient. Following

Cromwell's funeral in November 1658, his body would not be left in peace for long. The tensions between the army and civilians that had been so apparent at Cromwell's funeral would continue to plague the Protectoral regime. By May 1659, Oliver's son Richard Cromwell, or 'Tumble-down-Dick' as he would be disdainfully called, was effectively overthrown by a military coup at the hands of his brother-in-law Charles Fleetwood. Less than a year later, tired of unbridled and chaotic military government, Parliament invited back Charles II, thereby restoring Stuart monarchy. By January 1661, Cromwell was no longer lying silent with the kings of England, but hanged from the gallows at Tyburn to the jeering shouts of the London populace.

This was just the beginning of the adventures of Cromwell's head. During the next 300 years, it would travel from a traitor's pole on Westminster Hall to a number of museums, shows and even a Victorian breakfast table. It would be thrown from a building, concealed in a chimney and bought and sold numerous times. Along the way, Cromwell's head would encounter an opportunist soldier, a drunken actor, a money-grabbing publicist and forensic scientists, not to mention a gaggle of both amazed and sceptical onlookers. It captivated all who gazed upon it and, like the man it once belonged to, had the uncanny ability to provoke much debate. Indeed, the fortunes of the head mirrored each generation's attitude towards Cromwell. His reputation fluctuated through the ages, with some notable exceptions—such as the perpetual hatred of Cromwell in Ireland. In England, however, he would move from Restoration villain to Victorian hero, not to mention all the shades in between. Concurrently, attitudes towards his head would transform from a grizzly warning into a fascinating curio and sacred relic.

The journey from Westminster Abbey to Sidney Sussex, Cambridge was a long and incredible affair, the truth of which is often stranger than fiction. This is equally true of the man behind the head. A man who rose from country farmer to national leader cannot fail to attract attention. Yet how much do we know about the *real* Oliver Cromwell? The myths and legends that surround him provide a thick, if not impenetrable, smokescreen. For a man who is famously reputed to have asked to be portrayed 'warts and all', Cromwell still remains an enigma.

* I *
Tyburn and Beyond

As DAY BROKE on the cold winter's morning of Wednesday 30 January 1661, the crowds were already bustling around Tyburn gallows. Underneath the long shadow of the infamous 'Triple Tree', thousands would gather in anticipation of the day's events. This site, which had seen the death and destruction of so many criminals, was about to add a fresh chapter to its bloody history: the execution of Oliver Cromwell, Henry Ireton and John Bradshaw. Yet this would be no ordinary execution since all three of the condemned had been deceased for quite some time. Cromwell had now been dead for over two years; his son-in-law Henry Ireton had succumbed to a fever while on campaign in Ireland in November 1651; John Bradshaw, famous for his role as Lord President of the High Court of Justice that tried Charles I, passed away 15 months earlier in October 1659. Lying in their opened coffins, still wrapped in the cloths in which they had been buried, these 'three bold traitors' were drawn on sledges along the streets from Holborn to Tyburn. As they made their steady progress to the gallows, they were accompanied by the jeers and cries of the crowds that lined the route. The dawn departure and use of the coffins was a deliberate ploy to shield the carcasses from premature harm at the hands of overzealous bystanders. Arriving just after nine, the bodies were 'pull'd out of their Coffines and hang'd at the several angles of that Triple Tree' with their faces turned to Whitehall.[1]

Perhaps this outcome would not have come as a total surprise to Oliver Cromwell. At the height of his powers as Lord Protector, he had reputedly said of a cheering crowd that 'the people would be just as noisy if they were going to see me hanged'. Indeed, Cromwell had managed to draw in some considerable crowds during his tenure as supreme magistrate of the British Isles—not least the thousands who lined the streets at his funeral. Yet, a little over two years later, as Oliver had predicted, the crowds turned up just as willingly to witness his public execution.

The grisly puppet show was made all the more horrific by the advanced state of decomposition of the three bodies. A Spanish merchant named Samuel Sainthill gives a lurid eyewitness account:

The odious carcases of Oliver Cromwell, Major General Ireton, and Bradshaw, were drawn in sledges to Tyburn, where they were hanged by the neck, from morning till

four in the afternoon. Cromwell in a green-seare cloth,
very fresh, embalmed; Ireton having been buried long,
hung like a dried rat, yet corrupted about the fundament.
Bradshaw, in his winding-sheet, the fingers of his right
hand and his nose perished, having wet the sheet through.[2]

Bradshaw had died the most recently and, unlike Cromwell and Ireton, his body had not been embalmed, thus
accounting for the putrid stench that filled the nostrils of
the spectators. Peter Mundy, another witness to the gruesome tableau, noted how:

The bodies of Cromwell, Ireton and Bradshaw were
drawne from Westminster on sleads to Tiburne and there
hanged on the three partes of the gallowes. Cromwell and
Ireton wrapped in searcloth supposed to be embalmed, but
Bradshaw in a winding sheete. The body turned to putre-
faction sent a most odious scent all the way it went.[3]

For the Royalist Secretary Edward Nicholas, this was a
wonderful scene. Writing a couple of days later, in a letter
now held in the National Archives (see plate 5), he would
recall how, 'That Arch Traytor Cromwell & two of his
choicest instrum[en]ts Bradsh[aw] & Ireton finished the
Tragedy of their Lives & Our miseryes in a Comicke
scene. A wonderfull example of Justice'.[4] That one could
find comedy in such an act seems remarkable. Perhaps it
was the absurd futility of the actions inflicted upon these

lifeless bodies, rather than the nature of the act itself, which Nicholas found most ridiculous. He remained convinced, however, that what he saw was indeed a justified act of retribution as well as a crowd pleaser. He enthusiastically told another correspondent how 'the corpses of Cromwell, Bradshaw, and Ireton were dragged on sledges to Tyburn, remained hung on the gibbet in view of thousands, attracted by so marvellous an act of justice'.[5]

In comparison with Cromwell's lavish state funeral, this horrific defilement of the late Lord Protector's body marked an astonishing reversal of fortunes. The diarist John Evelyn, in a highly ecstatic mood, made the obvious contrast in his entry for 30 January:

> This day (O the stupendous and inscrutable judgements of God!) were the carcasses of those arch-rebels, Cromwell, Bradshaw (the judge who condemned his Majesty), and Ireton (son-in-law to the Usurper), dragged out of their superb tombs in Westminster among the Kings, to Tyburn and hanged on the gallows ... thousands of people who had seen them in all their pride being spectators ... look back at November 22: 1658 and be astonished.[6]

As the sun's glow began to sink behind the London rooftops, the dark finale of this grotesque pageant was acted out. After hanging from the gallows for around six hours, the bodies were cut down.[7] One by one, the heads were hacked away from the bodies and held aloft to the braying crowds. The unskilled butchery and layers of cerecloth meant that it took eight cuts before Cromwell's head was finally severed, the force of the blows knocking out several teeth and seriously disfiguring the nose. The barbarism did not stop there. It seems there was a ready demand for hideous souvenirs of the day's events. Sainthill describes how Bradshaw's toes were also cut off by the prentices and passed around the crowd—he himself holding 'five or six'.[8] The missing ear on Cromwell's head may also have been purloined in the same frenzied fashion.

With the work of the executioner complete, the headless trunks were thrown into the deep pit underneath the gallows, still swathed in their burial clothes. For their heads, however, there would be one final indignity. Attached to 20-foot tall oak poles, transfixed by metal spikes, they were to be placed on the roof of the south side of Westminster Hall (see plate 6). The location was no accident; this was the building in which the three men had given judgement against Charles I in 1649. Bradshaw, owing to his role as president of that court, was given the most prominent position of the three heads. According to one newspaper report in early February 1661, 'The heads of those three notorious regicides, Oliver Cromwell, John Bradshaw, and Henry Ireton are set upon poles on top of Westminster Hall, by the common hangman; Bradshaw is placed in the middle ... Cromwell and his son-in-law Ireton on both sides of Bradshaw'.[9] Samuel Pepys noted seeing the heads 'set up at the further end' of Westminster Hall on 5 February.

Staring out high above the London skyline, visible from miles around, the gruesome heads were an unmistakable and potent warning to all who viewed them.

* * *

This monstrous display was at a variance to the events of eight months earlier, when Charles II had returned triumphant to England. On 29 May 1660, his 30th birthday, Charles had entered the capital to the sight of bonfires and the sound of bells. Living on the Continent in exile since 1651, the king had now returned to claim his throne. Evelyn described the celebratory scene as 20,000 soldiers brandished their swords 'shouting with unexpressable joy'. The roads before Charles were strewn with flowers, tapestries were hung in the streets and the fountains about London flowed with wine. Yet the grisly events of 30 January 1661 were by no means totally removed from these joyous celebrations. A mood of retribution was already brewing among the populace. According to the Venetian resident, who personally witnessed these scenes in the capital, atop those numerous bonfires that lit the whole of London, the revellers were 'burning effigies of Cromwell and other rebels with much abuse'.[10]

Even before Charles II had set foot on English soil, the punishment of those who had been responsible for the death of his father was already under consideration. Although most of those who had strayed from the Royalist path during the past two decades would be given a general pardon, there were some notable exceptions. Anyone who was deemed guilty of 'execrable treason in sentencing to death, or signing the instrument [i.e. death warrant] for the horrid murder, or being instrumental in taking away the pretious life of our late soveraigne Lord Charles the first of glorious memory' was to be severely punished. In this act there was to be no distinction between the dead and living, all were equally culpable. To this end, Oliver Cromwell, Henry Ireton and John Bradshaw were 'convicted and attainted of High Treason to all intents and purposes as if they and every of them respectively had beene attainted in their lives'.[11]

Of the living, 49 men plus two unknown executioners were singled out for trial under the charge of high treason. Unsurprisingly, 20 of these men fled into exile at the king's return in a bid to escape their fate. Some did avoid detection; others were eventually found and brought home to face punishment. Of those who did not flee, 19 of them, although sentenced to death, were spared execution due to a combination of grovelling, influential political connections and royal clemency. Most would live out their days in prison. Perhaps the most fortunate of the regicides, however, was Richard Ingoldsby. Although he was a signatory to the death warrant, Ingoldsby had helped to quash military resistance against the king's return. As a result, Ingoldsby was added to the Act of Indemnity and was able to retain the estates he had required during the course of the Interregnum. Remarkably, he was even made a knight of the Bath at Charles II's coronation! His feeble excuse, that Cromwell had seized his hand and forced him to put his signature to the death warrant, was ridiculed but accepted. Not for the last time, Cromwell would become the scapegoat for others.

For the remaining 10 regicides there was to be no mercy, but neither did they seek it. Many of these men remained unrepentant to the last. John Cook, the principal prosecutor at Charles I's trial, wrote to his wife shortly before his death, adamant in the belief that 'We are not traitors, nor murderers, nor fanatics, but true Christians and good Commonwealth men, fixed and constant to the principles of sanctity, truth, justice and mercy, which the Parliament and Army declared and engaged for'.[12] Equally steadfast to his cause was the religious zealot Thomas Harrison. He told his judges that 'I do not come to be denying anything but rather to be bringing it forth to the light… It was not a thing done in a corner … I followed not my own judgement; I did what I did, as out of conscience of the Lord'. Harrison would be the first of the regicides to face the gallows and did so with a courage that must have shocked even the most ardent Royalists. The crowds were hostile to Harrison as he passed by 'Where is your Good Old Cause now?' they jeered loudly. 'Here in my bosom', replied Harrison, 'and I shall seal it with my blood'.[13]

Despite these 10 'king-killers' being hanged, disembowelled and quartered in late 1660 for their complicity in Charles I's death, the blood-thirst was still not totally quenched. In an impassioned speech to the Commons on 4 December 1660, the Royalist Silius Titus argued that 'since the Heads and Limbs of some were already put upon the Gates, he hoped the House would order the Carcasses of those Devils, who were buried in Westminster—Cromwell, Bradshaw, Ireton and Pride—be taken out of their graves [and] dragged to Tyburn'.[14] After a few days of debates and amendments by both Houses of Parliament, the Commons finally passed the following order on 8 December 1660 (the Lords giving their assent two days later), a copy of which is preserved among the State Papers at the National Archives (see plate 2):

> Resolved by the Lords & Commons assembled in Parliament that the carcasses of Oliver Cromwell, Henry Ireton, John Bradshaw, Thomas Pride, whether buried in Westminster Abbey or elsewhere be with all expedition taken up, and drawn upon a hurdle to Tyburn, and there hanged up in their coffins for some time, and after that buried under the said gallows: and that James Norfolke, Esq., Serjeant at Arms attending the House of Commons do take care that this order be put in effectual execution by the Common Executioner for the Country of Middlesex.[15]

In an eerie parallel to the events at Cromwell's death, a storm shook London on the evening of the Commons's resolution to exhume his body. Henry Townshend scribbled in his diary how that day was 'terrible windy like the day of Oliver Cromwell's death, and so all the week after'.[16]

Initially, no date was fixed for the execution of this Parliamentary order—only later was the symbolically important date of the regicide, 30 January, pitched upon. So 12 years to the day of Charles I's execution, these three notorious players in the events of January 1649 would finally be punished. The act of attainder, by which those 'guilty of the horrid murder of his late Sacred Majesty' were to be brought to justice, had included a provision for the 30 January of every year to be a 'Day of Fast and Humiliation'. In its inaugural year, however, this day of humiliation would be twinned with a less sacred act of cleansing past wrongdoings.

On 26 January 1661, Sergeant James Norfolke and his attendants, in pursuance of Parliament's orders, entered Westminster Abbey. Henry VII's Chapel, to the east end of the abbey, had become something of a Cromwellian burial vault during the Interregnum. During the Restoration, however, those members of Cromwell's family and circle who had made their resting place among the dust of ancient kings and nobles would be rudely disturbed.[17] The pompous monument erected to Cromwell had already been destroyed as early as June 1659. According to one newspaper:

> The stately and magnificent monument of the late Lord Protector, set up at the upper end of the Chancel in the Abbey at Westminster, is taken down by Order of the

Council of State and public sale made of the Crown,
Sceptre and other of the Royal Ornaments, after they were
broken. The Inscription set upon the wall is said to be thus:
Great in policy but matchless in Tyranny. It was put up by
one of the Royall party but pulled down by one of the
Souldiery'.[18]

Now Cromwell's burial vault was to meet a similar fate of
destructive fervour. Apparently, Cromwell's body was
hidden in the wall in the middle aisle of the chapel and
took some time to get at, owing to the several layers of
wood and lead that surrounded it. It proved heavy work:
John Lewis, the mason who was given the task of disman-
tling the stonework and removing the corpses, received
the sum of 15 shillings for his troubles.[19] According to
Thomas Rugge, a substantial crowd gathered in the chapel
to witness this act of desecration. Once Cromwell's vault
was opened 'the people crowded very much to see him,
who gave six pence apeece for to see him'.[20]

It was Sergeant Norfolke, however, who aimed to
make the largest profit out of the exhumation. When the
privy council had originally given orders for Cromwell's
burial in September 1658 they had insisted that:

his Highness [i.e. Cromwell's] Corps being embalmed,
with all due rites appertayneing thereunto, and being
wrapped in Lead, There ought to be an Inscripcion in a
plate of Gold to be fixed upon his Brest before he be putt

into the Coffin. That the Coffin be filled with odours, and spices within, and Covered without with purple Velvett, the handles, Nayles, and all other Iron Worke about it, be richly hatched with Gold.[21]

Uncovered for the first time since its burial, the coffin looked just as magnificent as the council had originally envisaged. Rugge noted how it was a 'very rich thinge very full of guilded hinges and nails'. Likewise the 'plate of Gold' was also there, fixed to Cromwell's body by a chain, and bearing a Latin inscription. Norfolke eagerly pocketed the plaque as a perquisite for his burdensome task. Only later, to his dismay, would he find that the Protectoral government had cut corners by making the plate from double gilt copper rather than solid gold![22]

The exhuming of both Cromwell and Ireton had taken quite some time. It was not until the evening of Monday 28 January 1661, under the cover of darkness, that their bodies were taken by cart from the abbey to the Red Lion Inn at Holborn. Bradshaw's body, perhaps because of its advanced state of decomposition, was not brought to Holborn until the following evening.[23] Strangely, Thomas Pride, another regicide who was to be exhumed and displayed at Tyburn on 30 January, was left in peace. The explanation for this last-minute reprieve is not clear, but given that he was buried at Nonesuch in Surrey, rather than Westminster Abbey, it may have been too bothersome for Norfolke to try and find the grave —

especially given the already time-consuming task of exhuming the other three regicides. Whatever the reason
for Pride's absence, by the evening of 29 January the
bodies of Cromwell, Bradshaw and Ireton were in place
at Holborn and ready to face their 'execution' the following morning.

*   *   *

But was the body laid out on a pub table in Holborn
actually that of Oliver Cromwell? Various conspiracy
theories have been propagated over the past 350 years.
Even among contemporaries, there was some dispute as
to whether the coffin interred at Westminster Abbey
actually contained Cromwell's remains. Others would
suggest that the body was substituted at its disinterment
and given a more honourable burial elsewhere—the terrible acts of Tyburn being inflicted on the substitute.
Alternatively, it has been insinuated that although the
body at the gallows was undoubtedly that of Cromwell,
his headless trunk may have been saved from the anonymity of the deep gallows pit and spirited away to a more
amicable location. Each of these possibilities warrants
closer investigation as only the latter would allow the head
on Westminster Hall to be that of Cromwell—the other
two suggestions necessarily turn 'Cromwell's' head into
an impostor: the anonymous head of an unknown victim.

As Cromwell's body lay peacefully on his deathbed at
Whitehall in 1658, the poet and Latin secretary for the

Cromwellian government, Andrew Marvell, was probably one of a privileged few to catch a glimpse of the late Lord Protector. In *A Poem upon the Death of his Late Highness the Lord Protector*, Marvell recalls the scene:

> I saw him dead. A leaden slumber lies
> And mortal sleep over those wakeful eyes:
> Those gentle rays under the lids were fled,
> Which through his looks that piercing sweetness shed;
> That port which so majestic was and strong,
> Loose and deprived of vigour, stretched along:
> All withered, all discoloured, pale and wan,
> How much another thing, no more that man?

The body would not sleep peacefully for long. By order of the Protectoral Privy Council the body was to be embalmed by three surgeons on the afternoon following Cromwell's death. They were to take care 'that the body be filled with Sweet odours, and the Service soe performed, that there may be noe danger of a Rupture afterwards'.[24]

In order to carry out both an autopsy and the embalmment, it appears that as well as opening up the body, the skullcap was sawn off to allow closer inspection of the brain (see plate 7). George Bate, one of Cromwell's physicians, gave a printed account of the process:

> His Body being opened; In the Animal parts the Vessels of the Brain seemed to be overcharged; in the Vitals the

Lungs a little inflamed … the Spleen, though sound to the Eye, being filled with matter like to the Lees of Oyls… Though his Bowels were taken out, and his Body filled with Spices, wrapped in a fourfold Cerecloath, but put first into a Coffin of Lead, and then into a Wooden one, yet it purged and wrought all, so that there was a necessary of interring it before the Solemnity of his Funeral'.[25]

One should not take Bate too literally. During the Restoration he would secure the position of physician to the restored king and was, naturally enough, keen to recount sensational tales about his previous master as a means to ingratiate himself with the new regime. Yet there is nothing in Bate's account to suggest that the body embalmed and buried was not that of Oliver Cromwell. With the embalming completed, the body was resealed and the skullcap sewn back on, the marks of the needle still visible on Cromwell's head.

It was not until 10 November 1658, however, that the body would be deposited in Westminster Abbey. Now more than two months since Cromwell had passed away, time was taking its toll on the corpse. There must always have been security concerns around the burial. According to the French ambassador, the government feared that disgruntled, underpaid soldiers, might 'arrest the corpse of the late Protector as security for their debt'. It was at one o'clock in the morning that the coffin was removed from Somerset House for its journey towards the abbey.

Passing through St James's Park in the darkness, accompanied by only a few mourners, this clandestine ceremony attracted few spectators. Upon arriving at Henry VII's Chapel, the coffin was privately interred there. This left the strange situation, whereby the grand state funeral for Oliver Cromwell, which took place two weeks later on 23 November 1658, replete with its standards, banners, trumpets and drums, would not actually involve the body of the person it sought to commemorate.[26] As the pageantry wowed the spectators crammed into the London streets, Cromwell's corpse already lay silent in the abbey. There it would lie until January 1661.

Nonetheless, some legends claim that Cromwell's corpse never rested in Westminster Abbey at all. One romantic tradition suggests that Oliver, shortly before his death, asked to be buried at Naseby 'where he obtained the greatest victory and glory and as near the spot as could be guessed, where the heat of the action was'.[27] Brought under the cover of darkness, Cromwell's body was buried by the midnight moonlight—the field being ploughed over the next day to ensure the burial location remained a secret. In a similar vein John Oldmixon, writing in the 1730s, claimed that a 'reliable Gentlewoman who attended Cromwell in his last sickness' had told him some years earlier how Cromwell's coffin had been thrown into the Thames in order to escape detection by the Restoration authorities:

She told me that the Day after Cromwell's death, it was consulted how to dispose of his Corpse. They could not pretend to keep it for the Pomp of a publick burial. Among other proposals was this one, that considering the Malice, Rage and Cruelty of the Cavaliers, it was most certain, they who never spared either Living or Dead in the Lust of their revenge, would insult the body of this their most dreadful enemy, if ever it was in their power; and to prevent its falling into such barbarous hands, it was resolved to wrap it up in lead, to put it aboard a Barge, and sink it in the deepest part of the Thames, which was done the night following.

Even more sinister is a story found by Pepys 'writ in a French book' in 1664, which maintained that 'Cromwell did, in his life time, transpose many of the bodies of the Kings of England from one grave to another, and by that means it is not known certainly whether the head that is now set upon a post be that of Cromwell, or one of the Kings'.[28] The story had a gruesome irony about it. Rather than hanging the body of Cromwell, the angry Royalists supposedly carried out a posthumous act of regicide upon one of the monarchs buried in the abbey. Some later rumours even made the astounding assertion that Cromwell had his own body substituted for that of Charles I, thus making an even greater mockery of the events of 30 January 1661.

Ultimately, these stories are merely good yarns born

out of over-active imaginations. If Charles I was the body desecrated at Tyburn, for example, one must wonder how the authorities went about hanging a body that had already been decapitated! More importantly, in 1813 the vault of Henry VIII in St George's Chapel, Windsor, was opened to allow a thorough examination of its contents. As expected, laid on top of the coffins of Henry VIII and Jane Seymour, just as it had been left in 1649, was that of Charles I. When the coffin was opened, the body found was unmistakably that of Charles—his facial features still recognizable, along with the tell-tale cut that severed the head from the body.

All these accounts of secret burial are deeply flawed because they are underpinned by the assumption that Cromwell presaged the desecration of his tomb after death. Yet, when Cromwell died peacefully in his bed on the evening of 3 September 1658, why should he have any inkling that two years later an angry reaction would seek to defame him? Moreover, if he feared some dark reprisals, why would he allow his mother, daughter and friends to be buried in the abbey? It is hard to argue with the answer Pepys received from Cromwell's former chaplain, Jeremiah White, when the former voiced similar concerns about a clandestine Cromwellian burial. According to White, Cromwell 'never had so poor a low thought in him to trouble himself about it'.

Of course, even if Cromwell's body was buried in Westminster Abbey in November 1658, this does not preclude the possibility of a substitution at a later date. With this in mind, the role of the pub in Holborn becomes particularly intriguing. Some have proposed that when the vault in Henry VII's Chapel was opened, to his horror, Norfolke found both the coffins of Cromwell and Ireton empty.[29] In their panic, the government sanctioned the exhumation of two anonymous graves to supply the places of the two regicides, heavily wrapping the bodies in cloths so as to complete the deception. Brought to the Red Lion Inn on 28 January, these bodies awaited the arrival from the abbey the next day of the only 'real' body to face the gallows, that of Bradshaw. An alternative theory, also centred on Holborn, posits that the body brought to the Red Lion was indeed that of Cromwell, but that friends of the late Protector managed to bribe those guarding his body (including Norfolke) into substituting it for another. Writing in 1787, the gossip-mongering John Prestwich propagated a rumour that Cromwell's remains 'were privately interred in a small paddock near Holborn; in that very spot over which the obelisk is placed in Red Lion Square'.[30] By this theory, when the sledges were dragged away by dawn's early light on the morning of 30 January, Cromwell's corpse was already safely buried.

The major flaw in this conspiracy is the fact that so many people *did* see Cromwell, Ireton and Bradshaw hanging from the Triple Tree that day—nobody suspected anything to the contrary. Cromwell, such a high

profile figure during the past two decades, was not somebody who could be easily mistaken. His distinctive facial
features, including his trademark warts, could not be
easily replicated. Admittedly, some eyewitnesses remarked
on how the bodies of Cromwell and Ireton were mostly
concealed, being wrapped tightly in cerecloth. Yet their
faces, at least, would have been distinctly visible to the
spectators—especially when their heads were held aloft
following decapitation. For these conspiracy theories to
work a crowd of thousands would have had to be com-
plicit; not one contemporary at the time mentioned the
notion that the body at Tyburn was not that of Cromwell.

A more probable tradition is that Cromwell's headless
body was recovered after the Tyburn affair and buried
elsewhere. One such tale is attributed to Cromwell's
daughter, Mary, who married Lord Fauconberg in 1657.
It is possible that Mary, securing her father's body from
the ignominy of burial in the common pit, had it buried
at her husband's country home of Newburgh Priory in
Yorkshire. The mystery surrounding this location's claim
to be Oliver's final resting place is enhanced by a tantaliz-
ing sealed stone vault in the priory that purports to contain the Protector's headless body. Unfortunately,
generations of owners of Newburgh have refused all re-
quests, including one from a curious King Edward VII, to
check whether there is a headless body lurking within. At
the same time, one must wonder how easy it would have
been to rescue Cromwell's body from the Tyburn pit

in the first place. Most accounts stress that the trunks of Cromwell, Ireton and Bradshaw were immediately 'thrown into a deep hole under the gallows' after their decapitation. Locating and removing the body, not to mention taking it on the long journey north, would have been no easy task. This story, like the others, is best confined to the realms of folklore.[31]

All things considered, it is difficult to refute the claim of one contemporary pamphleteer who stressed that Cromwell 'hath now no other Tombe but a Turf under Tyburn'.[32] There can be little doubt that Cromwell was indeed buried in Westminster Abbey in November 1658; equally it is highly unlikely that his body was substituted for another before the vile ceremony of 30 January 1661. No matter how much disgruntled Roundheads and paranoid Cavaliers might deny it, the Tyburn affair did succeed in meting out its loathsome justice on the intended victims. Despite numerous sites, stretching from London to Yorkshire, claiming to be Oliver's final resting place, the most plausible location remains under the Triple Tree at Tyburn—near the site of modern day Marble Arch. Thus, in 1661, Cromwell's body was consigned to oblivion. His head, however, continued to remain in the public gaze for quite some time.

* * *

This horrendous act seems to belie any notion of the Restoration marking the start of some idealized 'Merry

England'. Yet, at the same time, it was a necessary con-comitant of the king's return. Somebody needed to be blamed for the events of the intervening years, which had seen not only Civil War in three kingdoms, but also regi-cide, accompanied by the abolition of both the House of Lords and the monarchy. Thomas Rugge cynically attrib-uted this wave of revulsion against the late Lord Protec-tor to the age-old maxim that 'men in great power (right or wrong gotten) are admired, but once fallen from that are the most despisable men that are'.[33]

In many ways, exhuming and 'executing' Cromwell and his fellow 'traitors' was a form of national therapy. It served to create a few notorious 'scapegoats' onto whom everybody could project their collective guilt. The fact is, throughout the Interregnum—especially during the later 1650s—the majority of the country had started to grow comfortable under Protectoral, kingless, rule. Conservative gentry returned to the county benches; laws and proclamations emanating from the Protector and his council were generally obeyed; in short, life went on. Anybody who had lived peaceably through the Cromwellian age had, at least tacitly, conspired to keep the 'rightful' monarch away. With the king restored to the throne, a significant gesture was needed—not just bonfires and bells, but a real act of penitence, even sacri-fice, through the mutilation of the bodies of Cromwell, Ireton and Bradshaw.

For ardent Royalists, however, the Tyburn affair must

have been frustrating. It was standard practice in early modern England for the criminal, prior to execution, to give a final speech to the crowds gathered to watch their grisly end. Typically, the speech would contain a confession of their wrongdoings and give a nod towards the legitimacy of the punishment. It provided 'closure' on the process by demonstrating that justice had been correctly done. Yet the simple fact remains—corpses could not talk. Cromwell, Ireton and Bradshaw remained silent throughout the despicable acts carried out on their bodies. There would be no grand act of contrition on the steps of the gallows, no show of remorse for past transgressions. Indeed, the whole process of executing the regicides, both living and dead, had backfired. Most had gone to the gallows as martyrs, still defending the justness of their cause. Samuel Pepys would note with amazement the execution of a further three regicides in 1662: 'They all looked very cheerful, but I hear they all die defending what they did to the King to be just, which is very strange'. With the condemned either denying the charges against them to the last or, in the case of the dead, saying nothing at all, the meaning of the executions at Tyburn remained highly ambivalent.

One contemporary pamphlet even tried to put words into the mouths of the lifeless bodies of the three regicides. Entitled *The Speeches of Oliver Cromwell, Henry Ireton, and John Bradshaw, Intended to have been spoken at their Execution at Tyburne, Jan 30. 1660*, this tract provided a bawdy look at what Royalists believed should have been said beneath the Triple Tree. As Cromwell strides out before the crowds assembled about the gallows he admits the need to address his audience, 'it being a thing commonly expected at this place to speak something; I shall not break that good old custom'. The speech given is full of lurid details and no doubt reflects Royalist fantasies rather than political realities. Cromwell is portrayed pondering over past sins but, rather than repenting, seems to revel in them: 'For my part I followed alwaies Gentlemens exercises; Swearing, Whoreing, Drinking, and other the like commendable qualities, while I was a young man; When I grew more in years, I grew more cunning, and having play'd the Fool's part before, I play'd the Knaves now'. This comic caricature of Cromwell in some way undermines the grotesque reality of what really occurred at Tyburn. Yet, joking and mockery aside, one cannot help but feel that the impact of Cromwell's exhumation had provoked serious problems for the Royalists themselves.

The disinterment of Cromwell, Bradshaw and Ireton was certainly a double-edged sword. Arguably it brought onto the political stage the very person who the regime had sought to forget. The events of 1649 overshadowed the reign of Charles II. Despite the rapturous shouts and shows of affection on the king's return, Stuart monarchy at the Restoration could not simply pick up where it had left off in the 1640s. The climate had changed; the mystique of monarchy had been removed with the same blow that had severed Charles I's head. Drawing attention to the regicides and their notorious deed merely served to highlight this uncomfortable truth.

Moreover, Cromwell's revival in popular print, coupled with the exhumation of January 1661, literally brought him back from the dead. A number of satirical 'ghost pamphlets' poured off the London printing presses in the early 1660s, giving make-believe accounts of Cromwell's ghost wandering the earth, or languishing in Hell, while contemplating the acts he had committed in his own lifetime. The aim of this literature was not to scare or horrify but to amuse and titillate. It also mirrored the vulgar acts perpetrated against the bodies of the three regicides. In *A Parly between the Ghosts of the Late Protector and the King of Sweden*, published a few months after Cromwell's exhumation, Oliver is depicted quite comfortable in Hell, 'taking Tabacco in the great Divells own Closet'. Yet, even in the underworld, Cromwell could not be content, and attempts to overthrow Satan himself. His reward for this act of sedition was to be chained up 'before the General pissing place next the Court Door, with a strict charge, that nobody that made water thereabouts, should pisse any where, but against some part of his body'. Through the use of coarse and lewd language, Royalists tried to 'laugh-off' Cromwell's memory by turning him into a ridiculous clown-like figure.

Likewise, broadside ballads were printed and sung that

aimed to anaesthetize the vile reality of what passed at Tyburn. *The Last Farewell of Three Bould Traytors* sees Cromwell, Bradshaw and Ireton dancing off from Tyburn, bound for Hell, to a popular tune:

> Cromwell, Bradshaw, Ireton, farewell,
> with a fa, la, la, la, la, lero.
> A mess under Tyburn for the Devil of hell,
> with a fa, la, la, la, la, lero.
> From Tyburn they are bid adieu.
> And there is an end of a Stincking crew,
> I wish all may to their King prove true,
> with a fa, la, la, la, la, lero.

The final line betrays the anxieties of those who composed the ballad. With Cromwell exhumed and buried, it was time to move on and return to being loyal subjects once more. The government newspaper *Mercurius Publicus* summed up the mood in conclusion to its report on the events of 30 January 1661. With justice served on Cromwell, he was now 'thrown under the Gallows (never more to be digg'd up) and there we leave him'.

Such sentiments were wishful thinking. A head suspended 20 feet in the air from the roof of a prominent civic building would, quite literally, cast a long shadow. Nobody who walked beneath it could help but catch a glimpse of its ghastly gaze and recall forbidden memories. The ruthlessness and coarseness of Royalist attacks on

Cromwell provoked revulsion among many civilized men. Perhaps the diarist Samuel Pepys was not alone in thinking of Cromwell that 'it doth trouble me that a man of so great courage as he was should have that dishonour, though otherwise he might deserve it enough'.[34] Attempts to ridicule Cromwell, belittle his achievements, pour scorn on his character and physically destroy his person could not eradicate him from the people's thoughts. Perched high over the London rooftops, Cromwell would continue to loom over the Stuart monarchy for some time to come.

*   *   *

Well-weathered through its exposure to the elements, Cromwell's head remained defiant against the burning hot summers and bitter cold winters. Even the stonework on which the head was fixed proved less resilient. In July 1681, after over 20 years in the public gaze, Oliver's head was given a brief respite as workmen subjected the roof of Westminster Hall to repairs. One wit pondered 'whether old Noll's head did not take it for an affront to be thrown down from the pinacle of Honour, which is repairing at the South End of Westminster Hall'.[35] This affront was only temporary, however, and the head was swiftly re-placed. While Charles II sat on the throne, there was to be no reprieve for his old adversary.

Moreover, the head attracted fresh company in June 1684. Following the government's retributions in the

wake of the Rye House Plot, a failed attempt to assassin-
ate both Charles and his brother, a new wave of executions would ensure the Triple Tree kept busy. The death
of one conspirator, Sir Thomas Armstrong, who was
hanged, drawn and quartered at Tyburn, was recounted
in a newspaper report:

> He [Sir Thomas] was executed at Tyburn on Friday the
> 20th of June ... His Head was set on Westminster Hall
> between those of Cromwell and Bradshaw; one of his quar-
> ters upon Temple Bar, two others at Aldersgate and Aldgate,
> and the fourth was said to be sent down to Stafford, for
> which Town he had been a Burgess in Parliament.[36]

Nearly a quarter of a century after the Restoration the
gruesome executions continued to punish those who
sought an alternative to Stuart monarchy.

Whether Cromwell's head stayed in its lofty position
long enough to see the downfall of the Stuart dynasty is
hard to say. It seems to have remained exposed even after
Charles II lay dead and buried in 1685. Anecdotal evidence
claims that the head finally came down one evening in the
midst of a great storm that battered London towards the
end of the reign of James II. Again, it was the materials
around Cromwell's head, this time the oak pole that pro-
jected it into the sky, rather than the head itself, which
gave way. The pole snapping near the top, the head was
catapulted by the howling winds over the rooftops of

nearby buildings. Down below, beneath the south end of Westminster Hall, stood a solitary sentinel, doing his best to guard the nearby Exchequer Office in spite of the fierce weather. Landing with a thud near his feet, the soldier must have wondered how much more debris was going to shower down on him during the gale. Imagine his surprise then, when he found that this was no mere piece of building material—to his amazement, staring up at him, was a very familiar face.

Realizing the importance of his find, the guard acted swiftly. Even more than 25 years after the Restoration, this item was still notorious. Stories differ as to what happened next. By one account, retold over a century later, the soldier 'took it up with the broken spike in it, and carried it home'.[37] Another version of the tale gives a greater sense of the danger facing the holder of this ghoulish object. Apparently, the sentinel:

> perceiving what it was, placed it under his cloak till he went home; there he hid it in the spacious chimney of his room without acquainting his wife or daughter of the circumstance. Having concealed it for two or three days before he saw the placards which ordered any one possessing it to take it to a certain office, he was afraid to divulge the secret.[38]

All of London was on the look out for the head, hoping to claim the 'considerable reward' for its safe return. The sentinel, on the other hand, was equally aware that a severe punishment awaited anyone who had taken and concealed it, and therefore remained tight-lipped. Cromwell's head, so prominent for the past few decades, now waited in obscurity, believed by most to be lost forever.

Only on his deathbed, sometime at the turn of the century, did the soldier finally reveal to his daughter the secret hiding within the chimney. The most common tradition is that the sentinel's daughter, not entirely grateful for her rather unusual inheritance, decided to sell it on. Her husband went out looking for the best market for this strange item. Probably a number of collectors of curiosities, as well as relatives of the long-dead Protector, were approached in the process, yet no concrete evidence survives. With the head once more in the open, its history becomes somewhat hazy during the early part of the eighteenth century.

Not until 10 years later, in 1710, was the first firm sighting of Cromwell's head recorded since its disappearance from Westminster Hall. By then the owner of the head was not a relative of the sentinel, but one Claudius Du Puy, a French-Swiss calico printer. Du Puy was a keen collector of the weird and wonderful. His private museum of curiosities seems to have enjoyed worldwide fame and was certainly capable of attracting visitors from the Continent. Along with the Tower and Westminster Abbey, it probably ranked as one of the top London attractions of its age. It was not, however, a museum in the modern sense. Its exhibitions were not strictly designed to instruct or edify, instead the cabinets were crammed full of strange items intended to attract the visitor's baffled queries and amazement. A flavour of the items on display there includes waxwork models, musical instruments, hummingbirds, marine animals and a section dedicated to strange footwear. The decayed head of Oliver Cromwell would seem a perfect accompaniment to Du Puy's varied collection. Perhaps the sentinel's son-in-law saw a potential buyer in Du Puy and sold it to him directly, but evidence of such a transaction has not survived.

Nonetheless, Oliver Cromwell's head did somehow find its way into Du Puy's possession. One of the foreign visitors to the museum, Zacharias Conrad von Uffenbach, gave a detailed relation of what he saw. In the second room of the museum, among numerous rare coins and exotic herbs was 'Cromwell's head, as it had fallen down, complete with the broken-off wooden pole' on which it had been displayed. For Du Puy, Cromwell's head was his star attraction. Even though he had four rooms packed full of oddities, he himself admitted that this was 'one of the most curious items' among his *curiosa*. He was also immodest enough to boast to Uffenbach about its value, claiming he could get as much as 60 guineas for it if it were to go on sale.[39]

The German traveller, for his part, seems to have been far from impressed by what he saw. He was surprised that 'this monstrous head could still be so dear and worthy to the English'. Its poor condition made him wonder about Du Puy's generous estimate of its worth. Indeed, Uffenbach was more impressed by an ancient mummified head displayed next to that of Cromwell's 'which to me ought to have been more dear' than the battered object flaunted so proudly by Du Puy.

Moreover, Uffenbach would be the first in a long line of sceptics to question the authenticity of Cromwell's head. He 'became very suspicious that there be a piece of wood in it (and that the head should have fallen down with it) as usually the heads of malefactors are not put on wooden but rather iron stakes'. His criticism is not altogether valid. Uffenbach had visited London Bridge just days earlier, and had there seen the heads of criminals displayed on metal spikes. He failed to appreciate that just because iron prongs were used at London Bridge in 1710, that this might not have been the same for heads displayed in 1661. In fact, through his own sceptical testimony, Uffenbach unwittingly confirms the authenticity of Du Puy's object. Cromwell's head had indeed been displayed atop Westminster Hall on a wooden pole (albeit tipped with a metal prong which was rammed inside the skull), part of which had fallen to the ground with the head in the 1680s. This fragment of the wooden shaft would still remain embedded in the skull when it was finally buried in 1960.

* * *

Within the span of some 30 years the significance of Cromwell's head had changed markedly. At the Restoration it had been an extremely potent warning to others, a grisly reminder writ large in the London skyline of the price of sedition. Even as the Stuart monarchy was on its last legs in the late 1680s, the head was still potent enough a symbol for a nervous soldier to hide it in his chimney for 20 years in order to escape detection. By 1710, however, attitudes had changed; partly the result of the decline of Stuart fortunes and the fading impact of the events of over 60 years previous. The Civil War passed out of living memory and into historical legend. The head was now a curiosity, something that was intended to amaze and excite, rather than shock and repulse. It had become a commodity that could be bought and sold; a museum piece that could be publicly displayed without fear of reprisals. Once a warning against treasonous intentions, the head had become something of a macabre curio, an interesting relic of a past age.

Du Puy would die a bachelor and intestate in 1738. From that point on, the head drifted back into hazy obscurity, failing to reveal itself again for around 40 years. Yet Du Puy would not be the last to perceive the value of owning Cromwell's head or to realize the potential interest that such an object could draw. By the late eighteenth century the head entered the limelight again for a fresh generation to gaze upon, scrutinize, debate and marvel at.

* II *
On Show and On Trial

WHEN CROMWELL'S HEAD finally re-emerged to-
wards the end of the eighteenth century, it found itself in
the hands of a most unlikely owner. Samuel Russell was a
failed comic actor who had turned to drink in his time of
despair. Having few possessions, selling most of what he
owned to fuel his habit, Russell led an impecunious life.
Yet he did have one treasure to fortify him against those
evil times: the head of Oliver Cromwell. Russell would
claim to be an ancestor of the Lord Protector, the head
supposedly descending through generations of his family.
Perhaps there is some truth in this. The Cromwell and
Russell families were connected through a number of
marriage alliances including the marriage of Oliver's
fourth son, Henry, to Elizabeth, the daughter of Sir
Francis Russell. How the head came to pass from Du
Puy's cabinets of curiosities to the Russell family is unknown, but perhaps Oliver's 'relatives' were seen as a

ready market for such a strange item following Du Puy's death in 1738. In any event, one cannot imagine the head coming into the ownership of anyone more contrary to Cromwell's own 'puritanical' demeanour. The head of a man who famously ordered the closure of alehouses, now found itself in the possession of a person who haunted taverns on a more than regular basis.

Russell's treasured item did not escape detection, however. James Cox, one time owner of a large museum in London, had his eyes on this curious relic. Now operating as a jeweller in the City, Cox had a most precious commodity, in which Russell was distinctly lacking—money. When Cox first clapped eyes on Russell, around the year 1780, he was exhibiting the head at a small ramshackle stall near Clare Market. Cox, immediately realizing the importance of what he saw, and sensing Russell's weak spirit, resolved to get the head for himself. According to a later account, Cox was:

> Struck particularly by the appearance of the embalmed head, and convinced by all the circumstances attached to it that it was the identical head of Oliver Cromwell, Mr. Cox offered Russell £100 for it; nevertheless, poor as he was, and considerably in debt, he refused to part with it, so dear to him was that which he knew to be the sacred relic of his great ancestor.[1]

Just how nostalgic Russell was about his item is uncertain. In his drunken bouts he would reputedly pass the head around his gathered company, leading to a great deal of misuse and irreparable erosion of its features. It is more likely that Russell would not sell at the amount offered. Cox would have to secure his prize through more subtle means.

Indeed, Russell was not totally averse to selling. Sometime around 1775, he travelled to Sidney Sussex College, Cambridge with an intriguing proposition for the Master, Dr William Elliston. Reaching into the bundle containing his meagre belongings, Russell 'produced to the Master of the College ... the head of Oliver Cromwell, which he conceived the Master might be disposed to purchase as Oliver was of that College'. How a drunken comedian came to believe the Master of Sidney Sussex would be interested in this item has a deeper explanation than mere intoxication. Elliston and Russell did have something in common: Elliston's nephew was an actor under the management of Samuel Russell's son. It was probably this nephew who advised his employer's father to have a quiet word with his uncle about this most unusual item. Yet the plan failed. Although Russell employed every ounce of his acting ability to spin Elliston a convincing story about the head and how it came into his possession, the Master was not interested: 'Dr Elliston imagining it might create some prejudice against him to have bought the head declined treating with the man for it'. It would be another 185 years before the like offer came about again.

Realizing that Russell's professions of emotional attachment to the head were merely an attempt at bargaining for more cash, Cox decided to play the long game with his all-too-willing victim. Little by little, Cox lent money to Russell in order to keep him in the insalubrious lifestyle to which he had become accustomed. Oblivious to the trap into which he was walking, by 1787 Samuel Russell had run up a debt of just over £100. Cox now had Russell exactly where he wanted him and decided to call in the loan. Unable to pay with cash, Russell had to give away his only item of any worth. The deed of assignment by which the head was transferred from Russell to Cox is now in the keeping of Sidney Sussex College, Cambridge (see plate 13). As well as the £101 already advanced by Cox, Russell was to receive a further £17 from the London jeweller. For this total sum of £118 (a staggering £12,000 today), Russell did:

> Sell, release, grant and confirm unto the said James Cox all
> that Scull or Head supposed to be the Scull or Head of
> Oliver Cromwell, to have and to hold the said Scull or
> Head unto and to the only Use and Behoof of the said
> James Cox his Executors Administrators and Assigns
> absolutely for ever free from and without any Interruption
> or Disturbance whatsoever of from or by me the said
> Samuel Russell.[2]

Costing £18 more than he had originally offered seven years earlier, by a combination of devious means and a little patience, James Cox had finally got what he wanted.

One has to wonder why Cox went to such lengths for Cromwell's head. Its dull, flaking, worm-ridden skin, pierced by a rusting iron spike was hardly as aesthetically pleasing as the sparkling, luxurious jewellery by which he made his living. Having sold his museum many years before, Cox could not have wanted this head for display. His real motives seem to have been purely financial. He certainly displayed greater business acumen than Samuel Russell. Cox told everybody he knew about his recent acquisition with an eye to increasing its value. Indeed, his purchase could not have come at a better time. As a revolutionary fervour swept neighbouring France, a new fascination for that original 'revolutionary', Oliver Cromwell, gripped the nation. Cox reputedly complained of 'the great number of persons who intruded themselves upon him for permission to see it ... [which] occasioned him to change his residence, and keep his removal a secret, and he will now show it only to persons who go with particular recommendations from friends'.[3] It was a fine example of high demand but only limited supply. By promoting the notoriety of his item, while at the same time only allowing a privileged few to glance upon it, Cox was inflating its value immensely. What had been a faltering sideshow on a dilapidated market stall just a decade earlier, had now become the talk of the town. Cromwell's head had become big business.

Cox bided his time and waited for the right buyer to

maximize his profits. In early 1799 the moment came and he sold the head to three brothers for £230—almost doubling what he had paid 12 years before. Before the deal was totally sealed, Cox had to spin a few more yarns in order to convince his purchasers. Seeing in the Hughes brothers the same streak of greed that had first drawn him to the head, Cox once more emphasized the popularity of the item they were buying. He assured them that 'the long undiscovered preservation of the head of that extraordinary man is a matter of admiration', it had passed though the hands of numerous men who revered the great Lord Protector, just as 'thousands do to this day'. According to Cox, the head was a crowd pleaser. Unlike the thousands that had gathered at Tyburn in 1661 to see it severed, comparable crowds would gather to look on the head in a more sympathetic, inquiring fashion. This was just what the Hughes brothers wanted to hear. Fortified by Cox's assurances, the brothers began preparations for what they believed would be the greatest attraction in the whole of London.

The head was to be displayed, along with a few other curious items of *Cromwelliana*, in a building on Bond Street. Money was to be made through the charging of an entrance fee. In order to make the show a success, and maximize profits, the Hughes brothers sought the services of painter, antiquarian and publicist John Cranch, who set to his task with great alacrity. Hundreds of posters and printed fliers were distributed up and down the City bearing the none-too-subtle heading:

THE REMAINS OF THE REAL EMBALMED HEAD OF THE POWERFULL AND RENOWNED USURPER OLIVER CROMWELL Styled Protector of the Commonwealth of England, Scotland and Ireland; with the original dyes for the medals struck in honor of his victory at Dunbar, &c &c —are now exhibiting at No. 5, in Mead Court, Old Bond Street. ADMITTANCE, and printed copy of a genuine narrative relating to the acquisition, concealment and preservation of the articles exhibited, two shillings and six pence.[4]

All visitors would be provided with a pamphlet, 're-searched' by Cranch himself, which gave a narrative of the head's extraordinary century-long journey. Just as Cranch took up his pen to write this account, however, a momentary panic set in among the owners.

In order for the show's success to be secured, they had to reassure the crowds that this was indeed the '*real* em-balmed head' of Oliver Cromwell. Yet, as Cranch delved deeper into the material, he started to spot inconsistencies and gaps in the story. Suddenly, an uncomfortable feeling dawned on Cranch and the Hughes brothers— what if James Cox had sold them a fake? How could they be sure that what they were looking at was not a hoax? The whole success or failure of the show rested on being able to verify the provenance of their item.

With some logic, the Hughes brothers decided that

the best way to prove that their item was genuine was to work backwards through its previous owners. Ideally, a chain of ownership would be discovered leading all the way back to the head tumbling from Westminster Hall. Yet as they made their inquiries the story became even more complex. Their first port of call was James Cox. In January 1799, one of the Hughes brothers contacted Cox directly in a letter written with expressions of mild curiosity—but with an underlying tone that was far more confrontational. Hughes wrote to know more of the 'disposal of the O[liver] C[romwell] Scull which was purchased of you as the original'. He wanted Cox to give his 'answers & observations' to a number of details that were troubling the current owners. In particular, he was interested to hear that a Dr Combe claimed 'that some years ago he saw a scull in Butcher Row which was shewn him as the real O[liver] C[romwell] scull and the doctor then concurred in that opinion & still does so'. The last thing that the Hughes brothers needed was for somebody to present a rival 'head' that would cast doubt upon their own. As such, they needed to know whether 'that exhibition [was] of the present head or did you ever hear of any other in Butcher row'.

The current owners were also worried about defending against rival claimants for their head. They implored Cox to tell them more about Samuel Russell and the deal he made with him in 1787, 'whether it was not with much reluctance & after a long poverty he parted with it'. Their fears were fuelled further by an incident that apparently took place later that year when Russell came looking for the head:

> He appeared once before the house in Bond Street, where the Head was exhibited, and drew a mob round him by declaring that the embalm'd head of his great ancestor was his property, and that he had been 'juggled out of it' by Cox, who had taken advantage of his poverty, had arrested him, and had clandestinely taken the head from him, when he, Russell, was in a state of inebriation.

It was as the Hughes brothers feared. Cox had swindled Russell and then sold the head on to them for a tidy profit.

In reply, Cox sent a memorandum that promised much but revealed very little. The all-important issue of how the head came into Cox's hands was touched on lightly. He merely gave a narrative of the Tyburn affair followed by a relation of how the head 'upon a stormy night … was blow'd down & picked up by a Republican in whose possession, & that of his family, it was preserved & kept from the knowledge of the public & remained so nearly to the present time'. This sketchy account is perplexing — the implication is that William Russell was a descendant of the sentinel who picked up the head that fateful night. Indeed, it seems that this is what Russell had led Cox to believe. He had told a slightly different story to Dr Elliston when he tried to sell Cromwell's head to Sidney

Sussex in the mid-1770s. Then, Russell had claimed to have 'married the grand daughter of this soldier, and as Dr Elliston humorously observed had Oliver's head to her portion'. It was a convenient story, but also an implausible one. It provided a neat, clear line of descent for the head, but failed to take into account the murky realities. Du Puy's ownership, for example, is conspicuously absent. Cox tried to convince the Hughes brothers not to worry about thorny issues of past ownership. The head had to be genuine, 'As there never was before a Prince or a Protector after being buried with Regal Honors taken out of his grave, hanged & beheaded as Cromwell was it proves to the greatest certainty that the head still in preservation is his real head'.

As convincing as Cox's defence was, it did not satisfy Cranch who was still struggling to construct a believable story for the paying crowds. 'I fear it would be held incredible', Cranch wrote to one of the Hughes brothers, 'that Mr Cox should never have known how R[ussell] came by the article, unless indeed we suppose it to have been obtained surreptitiously'. Cranch endeavoured to construct a watertight explanation of how the head came to be in the possession of the current owners, even if this meant having to bend the truth a little:

A plausible cause of derivation *must* be made out; and though that derivation in some instances may not have been perfectly consonant to the laws … yet it may equally avail for our purpose—be equally curious and interesting, and go equally to the point of the authenticity of the subject itself, to show that it got into the hands of some of the former owners by some indirect adventure.

In the end, for all his artistic skill, Cranch had to admit defeat and the brochure he produced for the exhibit (see plate 15) failed to resolve the issue.[5] Instead, it tried to downplay the head's misty provenance. Cranch evasively stated that 'the history of the head, from the period when it was first deposited with the Russell family, to the time of its coming into the possession of Samuel Russell, is not, for the present, attempted to be more particularly given'. He freely admitted that 'it has been hinted that, by some concealment, or other indirect practice, the title of some of Samuel Russell's predecessors to the property of this head, was not quite *regular*'. Yet this was not reason in itself for concern:

> The remoteness of such a transaction would render it
> wholly immaterial whether this report were true or false,
> on any other account than this; that it is certainly no mean
> evidence of the value of such a thing, that it was worth the
> risque of stealing, or of fraudulently concealing it.

Paradoxically, that the head may have been 'merely' stolen added to its authenticity rather than tarnishing it. Ultimately, however, Cranch deferred to Cox's way of thinking. That is, although the head's past might be a mystery its very condition was testament in itself that it was genuine, Cromwell's head having been 'the only instance known of a head cut off and spiked that had before been embalmed; which is precisely the case with respect to the head in question'. Although Cranch was wrong on one point—the body of Cromwell's son-in-law, Henry Ireton, had also been embalmed before it was beheaded—this was a defence that would continue to endure for the following two centuries.

* * *

All this would prove to be a wasted effort. The Bond Street exhibition was a catastrophic failure. Perhaps this outcome should not be too surprising. James Cox's claim that the head would attract 'thousands' of admirers was partly a fabrication by which to substantially increase the value of his item. For Cox the head was a commodity pure and simple, he was merely trying to secure the best price. Moreover, it is difficult to escape the conclusion that all the talk of contested ownership coupled with the claims of 'rival' heads would have taken its toll on the show's popularity. One must wonder if people would have been willing to pay the two shillings and sixpence entrance fee (the equivalent of just under ten pounds today) in order to look at an object that was rumoured to be fraudulent. The historian Mark Noble, for example, was highly sceptical about whether that 'pickled head displayed for a show' was genuine.[6]

Another, more plausible, reason why the Bond Street show flopped was because the owners of the head had a disagreement with their publicist. John Cranch, working tirelessly to both research and promote the head, had received no payment from the Hughes brothers for his labours. It seems that an acrimonious split occurred between the men, with Cranch taking with him all the paperwork concerning the head—including the deed of ownership between Russell and Cox. This left the Hughes brothers in serious trouble. Lacking both the promotional skills of Cranch and the documents to back up the authenticity of the head, it would have been difficult for the show to go on.

Mysteriously, but perhaps only coincidently, shortly after this disastrous show all three of the Hughes brothers died in quick succession. Each meeting a sudden death, the final surviving brother falling from his horse in an apoplectic fit, rumours spread of a curse upon all those who possessed Cromwell's head. Yet these superstitions did nothing to keep the crowds away. By 1813, the head was exhibited again, now under the ownership of the daughter of the last surviving Hughes brother. According to one commentator:

> The Head of Oliver Cromwell (and it is believed the genuine one) has been brought forth in the City, and is exhibited as a favour to such curious Persons as the Proprietor chuses to oblige: an offer was made this morning to

bring it to Soho Square to shew it to Sir Joseph Banks, but he desired to be excused from seeing the remains of the old Villanous Republican, the mention of whose very name made his blood boil with indignation.[7]

Even so long after his death, Cromwell, and his head, still continued to divide opinion.

Considering purchasing Cromwell's head for the Piccadilly Museum, William Bullock consulted Lord Liverpool about 'the propriety of exhibiting such an article'. Bullock's own opinion was that the head was 'a mere matter of curiosity uninfluenced by any political opinions respecting Cromwell's character'. The display would be a gruesome peep show detached from any meaning concerning the person behind the head. Lord Liverpool's blunt response was highly disapproving of such an item, 'stating the strong objection which would naturally arise to the exhibition of any human remains at a Public Museum frequented by Persons of both Sexes and of all ages'. The age of publicly displaying severed heads in museums had passed. This new wave of 'civilized' thinking drove Cromwell's head into private hands, only occasionally revealed for the benefit of a privileged few.[8]

*　*　*

For the final time, Cromwell's head went up for sale. In 1815, the Hughes daughter, frustrated in her attempts to sell her grisly possession to public museums, found an alternative buyer—Mr Josiah Henry Wilkinson of Kent. Cromwell's head would remain in his family for the final 145 years of its adventures. It seems that Wilkinson was proud of his acquisition and was all-too-happy to show it to curious visitors. Lovingly preserved in a small oak box, the head would be produced as a conversation piece at private gatherings of friends and family.

In March 1822, accompanying his sister, Fanny, to a breakfast meeting at his brother-in-law's house in London, Wilkinson could not resist taking his curiosity along with him. Maria Edgeworth, also attending the breakfast, wrote with amazement about what she had seen. It was, most certainly:

> Oliver Cromwell's head—not his picture—not his bust—nothing of stone or marble or plaister of Paris, but his real head, which is now in the possession of Mr. Ricardo's brother in law (Mr Wilkinson)—He told us a story of an hour long explaining how it came into his possession.

Wilkinson related all the 'extremes of horror and infamy' to which the head was subjected in the Restoration era. He recalled the underhand dealings of James Cox, dramatically adding how Cox had Samuel Russell 'arrested and threw him into jail'. With the narrative over, Wilkinson then turned to examination of the head. With various members of the audience taking it in turns to hold the head by the bit of wooden pole protruding from its base, 'the happy possessor lectured upon it compasses in hand'. It was both a gruesome and spectacular sight. 'A frightful skull it is', remarked Maria, 'covered with its parched yellow skin like any other mummy and with its chestnut hair, eyebrows and beard in glorious preservation—The head is still fastened to the inestimable broken bit of the original pole—all black and happily worm-eaten'.[9]

Wilkinson fervently tried to convince everybody that his item was genuine. Maria herself admitted that 'there is not at first view ... any great likeness to the picture or bust of Cromwell—but upon examination the proofs are satisfactory and agree perfectly with the historical description'. One-by-one, Wilkinson explained the distinctive features of the head:

> The nose is flattened as it should be when the body was laid on its face to have the head chopped off. There is a cut of the axe (as it should be) in the wrong place where the bungling executioner gave it before he could get it off... To complete Mr. W[ilkinson]'s felicity there is the mark of a famous wart of Oliver's just above the left eye brow on the skull.

Not all the guests shared Wilkinson's credulity. When comparing the head with a plaster replica of Cromwell's death mask, 'Captain B[eaufort] objected, or was not quite convinced, that the whole face was not half an inch too short'. Wilkinson did not take too well to any slur on his treasured possession:

Poor Mr Wilkinson's hand trembled so that I thought he
never would have fixed either point of the compasses and
he did brandish them about so afterwards when he was
exemplifying that I expected they would have been in
Fanny's eyes or my own and I backed and pulled back.

Despite this momentary breach in the hitherto convivial
atmosphere, the company departed 'in a chorus of conviction' that what they had beheld was indeed the head of
Oliver Cromwell. Lord Liverpool may have thought this
item unfit for public display, but it continued to draw
interested onlookers in private Victorian homes. It had
become a kind of parlour game, some defending the
head's authenticity and others putting it under a little
light-hearted scrutiny.

To strengthen his defence of the head's authenticity,
Wilkinson sought out as much information relating to
the head as possible. He attempted to make contact with
both James Cox and John Cranch in order to put together a clearer account of derivation. Apparently, his
search for Cranch was successful. In July 1819, Cranch
'waited on Mr Wilkinson' concerning his desires 'to confer with me about the head of Oliver Cromwell'. Cranch
told him all he knew about the subject, 'with which information he was highly satisfied'. Sensing Wilkinson's
excitement over the head, Cranch saw the perfect opportunity to sell on the papers taken as 'security' for his payment following the Bond Street debacle. Cranch stressed

to Wilkinson that those papers in his possession were 'important to his purpose', especially, 'the identical original assignment of the head from Sam Russell to James Cox Esq.' For the mere sum of seven pounds, Cranch was willing to 'deliver all these papers ... immediately'. Somehow, the deal fell through. When, shortly after, Cranch emigrated to the United States the documents were believed lost forever. Not until 1898 would Cranch's niece, residing in Boston, discover the Russell–Cox deed and sell it to the Wilkinson family. Yet, even lacking these vital documents, Josiah Wilkinson had gleaned enough information to make some sense of his possession. In 1827 he committed this narrative to paper; partly for record, partly as notes for his ever-popular front room lectures.[10]

* * *

Documentary evidence was not the only means sought to verify the head's authentic status. By the mid-nineteenth century, Cromwell's head had descended to Josiah's son, Mr William Wilkinson. By now, a real vogue for Cromwell had begun to grip Victorian England, fuelled in part by the publication of Thomas Carlyle's *Letters and Speeches of Oliver Cromwell* in 1845. For the first time, Oliver's writings and speeches were accessible in print for a wide audience to read and enjoy. Who better then, than this foremost authority on all things Cromwellian, to confirm the authenticity of the Wilkinson head? Wilkinson's friend, Dr Gully, was particularly desirous to arrange a viewing of the head for Carlyle. Writing in December 1848, Gully was convinced that: 'if anyone has intellect in beholding the head of our national political saviour, it is the man who has so well vindicated his life and character'. Carlyle, however, was uninterested in the head. He had already 'some years ago' gone to 'Camberwell to view what was said to be the skull of Cromwell' but realized it was a fraud. As for the head in Wilkinson's possession, 'He further questions the probability of a head, tho' of an embalmed body, being able to last 22 years of air & rain & then be recognisable'. Carlyle conceded that the best way to satisfy his doubts would be to see the head. That he remained highly sceptical, however, was demonstrated by the fact that he merely sent his amanuensis, Mr Chorley, rather than attending the viewing personally.

Chorley's findings were inconclusive. Writing to Wilkinson in early February 1849, he expressed thanks for being able to look at what he tellingly described as the remarkable 'relic'. He admitted that both the documentary evidence provided by Wilkinson, and the impression left by the appearance of the head itself were strong. Carlyle, however, had heard enough. In a brief letter to the journal *Notes and Queries*, he reveals his hostile view:

There does not seem the slightest sound basis for any of the pretended *Heads* of Oliver. The one at present in vogue was visited the other day by a friend of mine: it has hair,

flesh and beard, a written history bearing that it was
procured for £100 (I think of bad debt) about 50 years ago
… the whole affair appears to be fraudulent moonshine,
an element not pleasant even to glance into, especially in a
case like Oliver's.[11]

Carlyle wrote off Wilkinson's possession as 'the head of
some decapitated man of distinction', but definitely not
that of the late Lord Protector. Yet in his flippant dis-
missal of this item, Carlyle did not display the cool reasoning that one might expect from an historian of his
mark. Besides Henry Ireton, there is no documented evidence of a comparable series of acts being carried out on
an embalmed body. What other 'man of distinction' in
the past 200 years had been embalmed, disinterred, beheaded and then had their head transfixed to a metal-
tipped post? Without ever clapping eyes on the object,
Carlyle nonetheless rejected it outright.

Carlyle's strident criticisms, however, did herald the
beginning of a fresh stage in the adventures of Cromwell's head. It now started to come under a higher degree
of 'scientific' examination than ever before. From the late
nineteenth century onwards, the tests done on the head
were far more vigorous than the harmless questioning of
the Victorian parlour. Coming face-to-face with archaeologists, scientists and cranial detectives, the fate of
Cromwell's head rested in the balance.

* * *

Throughout the nineteenth century, a number of skulls would come to light claiming to be that of Oliver Cromwell. It seems that something of a cottage industry in the production of 'authentic' Cromwellian heads had developed. All of these were dangerous pretenders to Wilkinson's possession, and all, one-by-one, would be exposed as fraudulent. The most persistent threat to Wilkinson's claim to have the 'real' head, however, was a skull that had been on prominent display in the Ashmolean Museum, Oxford, for around 150 years. Only now would these two 'rival' heads come face-to-face in order to discover which was the fraud.

Writing to the then custodian of the head, Horace Wilkinson (grandson of Josiah), in 1875, George Rolleston, Professor of Anatomy and Physiology at Oxford University, expressed his doubts over the item in the Ashmolean collection. While the skull had 'often been measured and referred to' as belonging to Oliver Cromwell, Rolleston had 'never so referred to it, being unsatisfied as to its authenticity'. The museum catalogue account of the Ashmolean skull, written in 1720, bore some echoes of the real story of Cromwell's head, but with a number of interesting inacurracies:

> In the year 1672, Oliver's skull was blown off the north end of Westminster Hall down into the leads of the same, and taken from thence by Mr. John Moore... Sometime

after this he gave it to Mr. Warner, apothecary, living in King Street, Westminster. Mr. Warner sold it for 20 broad pieces of gold to Humphrey Dove, Esq... This skull was taken out of Mr. Dove's iron chest at his death in 1687 by his daughter, Mrs Mary Fishe of Westminster, with which family it hath remained until given to Mr. E. Smalterrall.[12]

Among the most obvious mistakes, this story neglects the fact that the heads were on the *south* side of Westminster Hall as well as the accounts that Cromwell's head was still sighted there as late as 1684, some 12 years after the Ashmolean tale claims it had blown down. Rolleston could smell a rat.

Hearing that the 'real skull' was in the possession of Wilkinson, Rolleston was very desirous to see this 'specimen'. By comparing the Ashmolean skull to Wilkinson's head, he would be able to assess which of the two was the more likely claimant. Only one head could truly be described as the head of Oliver Cromwell. Wilkinson willingly gave his assent. After a full morning of pouring over the fine details of both heads, including a full comparison with the museum's Cromwellian 'death mask', Rolleston came to his conclusion: the Ashmolean skull was a fake, Cromwell's head was undoubtedly in the possession of Horace Wilkinson. On his return to Oxford, Rolleston would re-catalogue the museum's erroneous item: 'No. 561, imperfect *cavaria* with a hole in the right parietal. Once supposed to be that of *Oliver Cromwell*'. The skull was swiftly removed from the museum's display cabinets and disappeared from view.

Episodes such as this only served to bring Cromwell's head into the public spotlight and even brought it to the attention of the world's press. *The New York Evangelist* would run a story on the head as a front-page feature in August 1884, billed by the journalist William Breed as an 'interview' with the Lord Protector. Indeed in the United States, Cromwell was still newsworthy; he was a 'great Englishman, if not the greatest of them all', a man who was reputed to have almost made America his home in the 1630s. On his arrival in London, Breed was disgusted by the numerous commemorations of Stuart kings throughout London 'at almost every turn ... on pedestal, in fresco, on canvas, in public square and picture gallery; while for Cromwell we look almost in vain'. Lasting memorials to Oliver were hard to come by in the capital.

Cromwell's head, however, was still a lasting testimony to the great man. Intrigued by such a fascinating opportunity to meet Cromwell in the flesh, Breed contacted Horace Wilkinson for permission to conduct his interview. Having received 'a very courteous reply with an invitation to his home', Breed sped excitedly to Wilkinson's house in the Kentish countryside. 'In due time' Breed reports:

Mr. Wilkinson brought into the room a handsome polished box, out of which he lifted the venerable oak box which enclosed the head when so many years ago it came into possession of his family. Out of this he lifted the head. Before, however, opening the box, Mr. Wilkinson presented a variety of documents, some in print and some in manuscript, the latter being the account written by his grandfather, carefully and minutely detailing the historic accounts and confirmatory circumstances in the case.

Breed patiently read Josiah Wilkinson's account of the head's incredible history, but his real interest was lurking in the oak box. He was amazed to see its hair, the rusted spike and what is more the 'place of the wart over the right eye is unmistakable'. This was the 'very face' of Oliver Cromwell. Although 'no smile passed over those features at my presence, neither did those lips utter a word of salutation', its very presence spoke volumes: 'There seems to be no reason to question the fact that the head of the Great Lord Protector remains still above ground, as a grim protest against the brutalities that desecrated his grave'. Even if the face did not smile, like Alice in Wonderland's Cheshire Cat, its impact did leave a 'persistent grin'; no longer a warning to others against would-be king-killers, but a vile reminder of the gruesome excesses of a paranoid monarchy. Breed thanked Wilkinson for his 'gentlemanly courtesy' and assured his readers that 'a similar reception awaits any other of our countrymen who would care to look upon so curious a relic'.

This media interest was a mixed blessing for Horace Wilkinson. A reserved, private man far removed from the extrovert nature of impresarios such as John Cranch or the greedy guile of James Cox, Wilkinson preferred to show the head personally to a few curious visitors. He cast himself as guardian of the head and was not keen to abuse his role. Over the course of the following decades, however, despite Wilkinson's attempts to keep his possession as low-key as possible, there was a growing tide of opinion that Cromwell's head should not be allowed to rest in its rural obscurity.

In 1895 the debate had once again spread over the Atlantic, finding its way into the *Pittsburg Leader*. Feeding off a fresh clutch of reports in England over the recent 'discovery' of the head in Wilkinson's possession, there followed a great deal of musing over the future of such an object. Mr Samuel Church, a historian residing in Pittsburg, had already advised the *London Chronicle* on the subject, but was all too willing to recount the tale to his native newspaper. Just as William Breed had complained a decade before, Church stressed the need for a lasting monument to Cromwell in the capital. Before this was built, Church believed there should be:

A committee of the greatest living experts on the Cromwell epoch to examine the Wilkinson head, and I named Prof. S.R. Gardiner and Charles H. Firth of Oxford, and Frederic Harrison, the famous correspondent and critic, of London.

> If they should find that there is no reasonable doubt against
> the authenticity of the Cromwell head ... it should be given
> burial under the Cromwell monument, and that then the
> Cromwell party the world over could look upon that as
> Cromwell's sufficient grave.

Not for the first time, there was a strange belief that historians rather than scientists were the best people to identify the 'real' head of Oliver Cromwell. Church was fully satisfied that his solution would bring closure on the whole affair. By putting it under this intense scrutiny, Church 'would not be surprised if, in the next year or two, this Wilkinson head is either rejected finally by competent opinion, or else accepted and buried under a splendid monument of bronze'. Neither outcome ever occurred. Despite the growing tide of interest in Cromwell, Wilkinson was not keen to relinquish his family heirloom to the public.

*   *   *

Not until 1911 would Cromwell's head be finally given the thorough examination so long called for. Somewhat ironically, the *Royal* Archaeological Institute were behind this fresh attempt to prove whether this was indeed the head of the famous king-killer. Its then owner, Reverend Horace Wilkinson, attended the exhibition with mixed feelings. According to the society's report:

Before reading some notes which had been written by his great-grandfather, Mr. Wilkinson desired the members to understand that although it had been in the possession of his family for four generations, the head had never been exhibited publicly since it had come into the possession of his family. It was no ordinary relic, and he would consider it very improper to keep it above ground if it were not treated with reference and respect. As this was a private meeting and the Institute a society of people who would look at the matter in a proper spirit, he had great pleasure in bringing it there that day.

Displaying the same amount of reticence as his forebears, Wilkinson only brought the head on the understanding that this would be a private affair. He wished to avoid any publicity—probably betraying nervous feelings over what the eminent panel of experts might discover.[13]

The first phase of the investigation involved a brief consideration of rival claimants. The Ashmolean head was given another airing in order to make yet another detailed comparison with the head in the possession of Wilkinson. Their findings differed little from what Rolleston had discovered 30 years before. Professor Bourne of the Ashmolean Museum assured the assembled company that the skull had 'long since lost all character of authenticity'. Indeed, that it was a hoax had become even more obvious by the fact that the hole in the top of the skull was the result of 'an instrument having been driven into it, not from the bottom, but from the top', meaning it was not the mark of the iron-tipped traitor's pole on which the real head would have been thrust. Nor did the skull have any 'trace of skin or flesh or hair to show that it had ever been embalmed'. Professor Boyd Dawkins was convinced that 'on craniological grounds ... the Oxford skull could not have been Cromwell's, both because it does not fit his capacity and because it appears to belong to a younger man'.

Yet, while the archaeologists categorically agreed the Ashmolean skull to be a fake, they were a little more guarded in their comments about Wilkinson's head. Not everybody was as forthright in their expressions as Dawkins, who declared the evidence regarding the embalmed head to be 'absolutely clear and distinct'. They had heard Josiah Wilkinson's account of 1827 concerning the head's provenance, and had laboriously consulted all the documents relating to the head in Wilkinson's possession, but some had lingering doubts about the unbelievable story. The Reverend R.S. Eld reminded his colleagues of a recent article by one Dr Welldon that 'objects altogether to the story of the Cox and Wilkinson head'. There was still a need to account for the 'gap between 1684 and 1787' during which time the head's whereabouts was largely unknown. Although for Mr Hope 'the historical evidence, after the skull passed into the hands of the actor Russell, appeared genuine enough', he could not ignore that 'there was a period of one hundred years to bridge over between the time when it was set upon … Westminster Hall, and the time when it comes to light again as the reputed skull of Cromwell'. If Wilkinson had the same disposition as his great-grandfather, one would have expected his hands to be trembling at this point.

These archaeologists were more satisfied with the relic itself than the story that supported it. Despite its murky past, one could not overlook the 'internal evidence afforded by the head itself'. Its appearance was the best testimony to its authenticity. As Eld argued, in a defence not unlike that made by James Cox in the late eighteenth century, Cromwell's head had 'undergone these three vicissitudes, unparalleled in the history of even royal heads, embalmment, decapitation and transfixment on a pike'. The head exhibited by Wilkinson showed all these signs. Moreover, it had clearly been severed *after* death and embalmment, as 'in an ordinary decapitation the skin shrinks, but in this case the skin has not shrunk after the strokes which severed the head from the body'. That the hair, which still sprouted from its withered skin, was a reddish colour quite unlike Cromwell's was not a significant problem. Professor Dawkins explained how 'in his experience there is a shade of red in all hair, even the blackest, but it is obscured by the black pigment; and as this fades the red shade comes further and further to the front'. The overall impression was that while the documentary evidence was slightly dubious, the physical evidence was extremely strong. Although it was not categorically proven that this *was* Cromwell's head, unlike the Oxford skull, there was no way the possibility could be refuted.

How Wilkinson took this news is uncertain. The results were not widely published perhaps reflecting Wilkinson's desire to keep the result a matter of secrecy. This could not quell the public fascination with Cromwell's head, however. To Wilkinson's horror, a picture of the head found its way into the *Daily Mail*, sparking a frenzy of letters to various national newspapers. In 1923 the magazine *Cassell's Weekly* printed an article with the bold headline 'The Head of Oliver Cromwell: Is the Wilkinson Relic Genuine?' The reporter, Mr Sheridan Jones, was shocked to hear that 'for over a century, it is claimed, Cromwell's head has been in the possession of a family named Wilkinson'. What is more, 'when the Royal Archaeological Society investigated the facts, Professor Dawkins declared that he had never heard of a more complete chain of circumstances'. The matter was of such importance, that it had been taken to the very top:

> These facts, or some of them, were pressed on Mr. Asquith while he was Prime Minister, and he was urged to secure the relic for the nation, 'the same to be buried with all reverence and respect'. But with characteristic caution, he replied that, so long as there was an element of doubt, this was impossible.

Sheridan Jones believed it was time to remove these uncertainties once and for all. If Wilkinson's relic were genuine it was a national treasure and belonged to the people—it should not lay hidden away. To prove its authenticity, Jones had been in contact with the 'eminent craniologist' Sir Arthur Keith who told him 'he could easily determine' if the Wilkinson head was Cromwell's. 'It only remains, therefore,' Jones concluded by means of a challenge, 'for the Editor of *Cassell's Weekly* to arrange with the Rev. H.R. Wilkinson to place the head in Sir Arthur's custody. Our readers will await the result, which we shall make known in due course, with great interest'.

Although Wilkinson refused to be goaded by this impetuous contest, the barrage of public interest demanding 'scientific' tests probably took their toll. In 1934 Canon Horace Wilkinson allowed his prized possession to be taken away by two eminent scientists: the eugenicist Karl Pearson and the anthropologist Geoffrey Morant. Their results were to be published both in the scientific journal, *Biometrika*, and in a special publication by Cambridge University Press. Unlike the findings of the Royal Archaeological Institute, the conclusions reached by these two men would be made widely known and therefore Wilkinson stood to seriously lose face if the results were not favourable. In their introductory, Morant and Pearson forcefully defended the need for a fresh study of the head:

> So much has been written about this Head, and the
> controversy has been so keen, that it might appear that
> there was nothing to be said on the topic which had not

been said already. In other words that the authenticity of the Head must be ever left in that state of doubt in which historians and critics have enveloped it.

For these two cranial detectives, however, such defeatism was unacceptable. Before now the head had only been subjected to the musings of antiquarians and the commendable, if a little lackadaisical, examination of archaeologists and historians. What Morant and Pearson offered was a rigorous comparison of the head with surviving images of Cromwell; they trusted 'solely to the measurements on the Head, and to its good or bad fit to portraits'. Unlike previous investigators they considered the head's provenance but were not so predisposed to obsess over it. Instead, they would seek to prove or disprove that the head itself 'fitted' the actual physical appearance of Oliver Cromwell.

As they analysed each detail of Wilkinson's head, the evidence became stronger and stronger. The embalming on the head was exactly analogous with what one would have expected from the mid-seventeenth century. The removal of the skull-cap, for example, 'was usual in all major and particularly in royal embalmments'. Still visible were the 'needle holes round the leather-like skin which indicate that the skull-cap had once been stitched on again'. Also the head was 'attached to an oaken pole, surmounted by an iron spike' just as one would expect, but even more convincingly:

The pole has been long in contact with the Head, for some of the worm holes pass through the Head and the pole. The spike where it has penetrated the skull-cap has rusted away, but inside the brain-box it has been less attacked… This prong has been so forcibly thrust through the skull-cap that it has split it from the place of penetration to the right border.

All but two of the teeth had fallen out since the death of the victim, moreover 'the nose of the Head inclines to the left cheek, but is too battered to allow us to assert any-thing about it'. These gruesome features all added up to strong evidence in favour of the Wilkinson head being that of Cromwell.

Of course, it was not beyond the realm of possibility that the head was a very good forgery. Here the patchy history of Cromwell's head before the late eighteenth century proved highly problematic. Without a doubt, Pearson and Morant could prove that the head before them in 1934 was the very same that the Hughes brothers had bought from Cox in 1799. Cranch's drawings and painting of the head from the time of the Bond Street show were almost identical to the head's condition over a century later. Yet it was less easy to prove that this was the same head that Du Puy had displayed in 1710, even more tricky to trace it back to the pole on Westminster Hall. If this were a for-gery, however, some of the lengths that the forger would have had to go to would have been incredible. The head had definitely been separated from the body *after* embalmment, for example, meaning that the forgers must have embalmed 'a large portion, if not the whole of the fresh corpse, and then proceeded to chop off the head with an axe in the crudest possible manner' in order to emulate the clumsy blows of the Tyburn executioner.

The fact that so many incidental features of the head complied so neatly with the story behind it, fortified Morant and Pearson in their conclusions (see plate 7). What forger would have been aware that the 'the skull-cap must be removed before, and the head chopped off and by several blows after embalmment?' Why would they have 'broken the nose, made the lips appear to be decayed away, left only two teeth in the head, and removed the hair' if they wanted others to be convinced that this was Cromwell's head? If it were a forgery, one would have expected the forger to make it look physically more 'like', that is more easily identifiable as, Oliver Cromwell. Instead, it took the keen eye of forensic scientists to actually draw out the features that marked out the head as genuine. Yet even if this head did 'contain much of its history in itself', that did not definitely prove that it was Cromwell's.

To get a more definitive result, Morant and Pearson turned to biometrics—examining the dimensions of Cromwell's head against those from portraits, busts and death masks. Portraits of Cromwell were first considered, but thought best avoided because of problems of scaling and proportion, not to mention various inconsistencies *between* the representations of different paintings. They then turned to 'truer' impressions of Cromwell's face including a bust of Cromwell from Florence (believed to be used to make his funeral effigy) and numerous 'life masks' and 'death masks' (impressions of Cromwell's face before and after death). Painstakingly measuring every facet of these representations of Oliver's face, they calculated a 'mean' or average of the dimensions of Cromwell's actual head (see plates 16–17). They then set about trying to compare this data to the Wilkinson head.

This was no easy task, as they freely admitted. While accurate measurements of a living head might be tricky enough, the matter was made even more complicated by the unequal shrinkage of the skin on the embalmed head. With these shrinkages factored in, however, the two scientists were extremely happy with their results: 'Considering the vagueness of the points between which measurements have to be made and the obvious liability to error, it must be admitted that the accordance between the mean of the masks and busts and the Wilkinson Head is astonishing'. The data was almost an exact match. Transposing the scaled image of the Wilkinson head onto the various death masks showed a very close fit—the telltale depression left by the wart, for example, matching perfectly with Cromwell's face.

All the evidence added up to make a compelling case. In their concluding remarks, Morant and Pearson had to admit that 'the defective history of the Head hinders the *demonstration* that it is Cromwell's'. But where history faltered, science was able to supply the answer. They had started their inquiry in an 'agnostic frame of mind', ignoring the numerous historical justifications used to claim the head's authenticity, trusting instead in meticulous scientific examination. After an innumerable amount of measuring, photographing, probing, X-raying and pondering (see plate 18) the duo realized the enormity of their painstaking efforts. By the end of their investigation, they had come to the conclusion that 'it is a "moral certainty" that the Wilkinson Head is the genuine head of Oliver Cromwell, Protector of the Commonwealth'. After nearly two centuries of speculating over authenticity, Cromwell's head had finally been given a categorical, 'scientific', seal of approval.

*   *   *

Ironically, shortly after Cromwell's head had finally been conclusively 'discovered' it would disappear forever. In 1957 Canon Horace Wilkinson passed away, bequeathing the head to his son, Dr Horace Norman Stanley Wilkinson. By now, Dr Wilkinson had evidently grown tired of the considerable interest that his inheritance generated. Despite the head being revealed as genuine, he was adamant that it should not be made into some kind of exhibit or freak show in the vein of Du Puy and the Hughes brothers. Instead, Dr Wilkinson seems to have resolved that the head should finally be given the decent burial that it had for so long been denied. Laid to rest for barely two years in Westminster Abbey, Cromwell's head had been travelling ever since. It was time for it to receive a much-needed rest. Considering the options carefully, as well as the need for a discreet, low-key burial, Wilkinson contacted Oliver's Cambridge college, Sidney Sussex, in early 1960. The establishment that had refused this curious relic over 150 years earlier, now warmly welcomed back their infamous alumnus.

By mutual agreement of the college authorities and Wilkinson, all media coverage was avoided for the head's final journey on 25 March 1960. The ceremony was to be a private affair attended by Wilkinson and his sister as well as a few representatives of the college including the Master, David Thomson. The head would be carefully preserved in the same wooden box in which Josiah Wilkinson had so proudly kept it in the 1820s. This, in turn, was sealed in an airtight metal container that was interred in a secret location near the college's antechapel. The clandestine service lasted barely half an hour and left no permanent memorial to the fact that it had taken place. In order to maintain complete secrecy, the plaque marking the burial was not revealed until over two years later, in October 1962.

Unaware of the fate of the head, debate still raged on about its future. Some looked on Cromwell's remains with anger not unlike the braying crowds of 1661. According

PLATE 1: A portrait of Oliver Cromwell after Robert Walker, *c.*1649. Cromwell is dressed in his customary 'plain style' of white collar and black armour.

Die Luna 10.die Decembris
1660.

Ordered by the Lords and Comons assembled
in Parliament, That the Carcasses of Oliver
Cromwell, Henry Ireton, John Bradshaw,
Thomas Pride, whether buried in Westm͠
Abbey, or elsewhere, be withall Expedition
taken up, and drawne upon a Hurdle to Tyburne, and there Hanged up in their Coffins
for some tyme, and after that buried under
y͠e said Gallowes. And that James Norfolke Esq͠ Serjeant at Armes attending y͠e
house of Comons, doe take Care that this
Order be put in effectuall Execution by y͠e
Comon Executioner for the County of Midd͠
and all such others to whom it shall respectively appertaine, who are required in
their severall places to conforme and observe
this Order with Effect: And the Sheriffe of
Midd͠ is to give his Assistance herein, as there
shall be occasion. And y͠e Deane of
Westminster is desired to give directions to
his officers of the Abbey to be Assistant in
y͠e Execution of this order.

Jo: Browne Cleric
Parliamentor͠

PLATE 2, *facing page*: A copy of the order of Parliament to disinter the carcasses of the regicides Oliver Cromwell, Henry Ireton, John Bradshaw and Thomas Pride, 10 December 1660. (TNA SP 29/23 f. 70)

PLATE 3, *right*: One of the many funeral escutcheons from Cromwell's elaborate hearse. The imperial crown above the coat of arms hints at the funeral's regal opulence.

PLATE 4, *right*: Oliver Cromwell's death mask. Created shortly after his death in September 1658, it features the famous wart above his right eye.

1. Cremwels haupt.   2. Bratshew.   3. Ireton

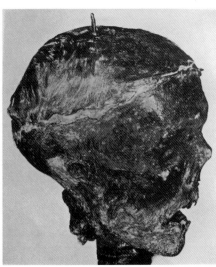

PLATE 6, *above*:
A Dutch engraving of
the gallows at Tyburn.
In the background is
a representation of
Westminster Hall,
complete with the
decaying heads of
Cromwell, Bradshaw
and Ireton.

PLATE 7, *left*: A
photograph of Oliver
Cromwell's 300-year-
old head, taken in the
1930s. Note the tip of
the iron prong piercing
the skull as well as the
cincture marking the
removal of the skull-cap
during the post mortem
and embalming.

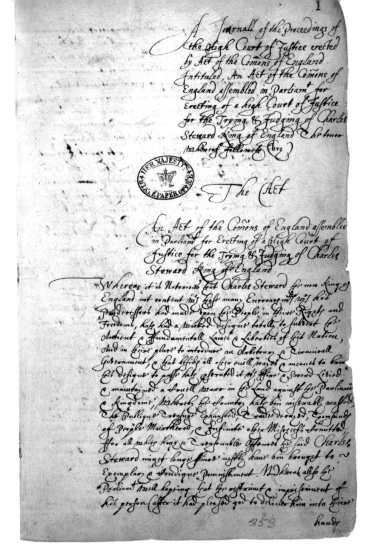

PLATE 8, *above*: The opening page of the journal of the High Court of Justice that tried Charles I, now held in the National Archives. The account opens with the Commons' Act to erect the court. Charles's charge was a weighty one—he was labelled the 'occasioner, author, and continuer of the said unnatural, cruel and bloody wars'. (TNA SP 16/517 f. 1)

PLATE 9, *right*: The list of commissioners present on 20 January 1649 at the opening of the unprecedented trial of a king. Note that the first three names are Bradshaw, Cromwell and Ireton, the high-profile regicides who were later 'executed' at Tyburn.
(TNA SP 16/517 f. 13)

PLATE 10, *below*: In this excerpt from the account of Charles I's trial, on 20 January 1649, the king demands to know 'by what power I am called hither' before answering any charges.
(TNA SP 16/516 f. 16)

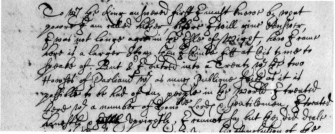

PLATE II: Sir Peter Lely's celebrated portrait of Oliver Cromwell, dating from the mid-seventeenth century. Cromwell supposedly told Lely to paint him 'warts and everything', warning the artist that otherwise he would not 'pay a farthing for it'. Such concern with plain speaking was typical of the man.

to one newspaper reporter, 'I have met people who would like to nail the head to the doors of the House of Commons as a permanent reminder to all who enter... There are others who wish to reunite the head to the body, but I know of no attempt to locate the body'.[14] The reasons for the secret burial were obvious. It would save the head from friends and enemies alike. Well-meaning admirers could prove just as dangerous as would-be Royalists out for 'revenge'. It was time to leave the head alone. It had undergone the rigorous probing of scientific study, withstood the gawping crowds of numerous peepshows and remained defiant against the bloodthirsty Restoration regime. Along the way it had met with both well-meaning protectors and scheming scoundrels. Now it had found peace. To this day Sidney Sussex College is the proud guardian of Cromwell's head, its true location a closely guarded secret known only by a privileged few. There it will continue for evermore enjoying its well-earned and long overdue resting place in Cambridge's tranquil surroundings.

* * *

Over three centuries since its eventful adventures began, Cromwell's head had finally reached journey's end. That it had taken so long owes a lot to the enduring reputation of the man behind the head. Cromwell continued to fascinate and intrigue as much in death as he had in life. Few figures in history have created the same intensity of debate as he has. By exploring Cromwell the man, and the subsequent legends and myths that came to envelop him in death, the remarkable afterlife of his head becomes a lot clearer. Even with Cromwell's head safely interred, his memory was not allowed to rest. Now some 350 years since his death, Cromwell lives on as a controversial figure.

* III *
The Mind is the Man

THE VILE EVENTS that took place at Tyburn on 30
January 1661, launching Cromwell's head on its 300-year
adventure, were a calculated act of punishment. Behind
the blundering butchery was an intense hatred for what
Cromwell and his allies had achieved during their life-
times. Although, legally speaking, the crime for which
they were posthumously executed was 'high treason', the
underlying charge was the heinous, unthinkable act of
king-killing. 'Regicide' was a most egregious sin: the
murder of God's anointed monarch. It is unlikely that
this fact escaped those who participated in the trial and
execution of Charles I in 1649. Indeed, because of the
personal risk, not to mention the political turmoil, that
the king's execution might entail, it was a decision that was
not taken lightly. It is too easy to be seduced by the post-
Restoration caricature of the power-hungry, hypocritical
Cromwell. In reality, as we shall see, Cromwell only

backed regicide as a last resort; it was a painful decision that fermented over many months of political turmoil and bloody warfare.

There is also an irony in the fact that Cromwell's head would be displayed above Westminster Hall. Although the location made sense, given that it was the building in which the regicides had sat in judgement over the king, it was also the very place where, in 1657, Cromwell was invested as Lord Protector with all the trappings of monarchy. Yet, earlier that year, Cromwell had refused to take the Crown when it was offered to him. The latter part of this chapter will seek to examine why Cromwell refused to become king. The decision provoked contrasting reactions from those around Cromwell—some would cheer while others would lament. How Cromwell himself would come to reflect on his decision is also worthy of examination. Perhaps the grisly events of 1661 would never have occurred had Cromwell accepted the Restoration of monarchy, albeit Cromwellian monarchy, three years earlier.

* * *

The mind is the man. If that be kept pure, a man signifies somewhat; if not, I would be very fain what difference there is betwixt him and a beast.[1]
Oliver Cromwell to Parliament, 17 September 1656

For Cromwell, it was the mind that made the man. Once dead and the soul departed, the body signified nothing more than a vessel. In this way, the Tyburn affair and the despicable acts committed on his corpse would have meant little to him. To understand Cromwell in life, however, and why his head ended up planted on a pole in death, it is essential to get inside his head: to examine how his mind worked. Cromwell's way of thinking was never quite straightforward; his paradoxical nature—a combination of conservative gentleman and godly radical—produced a great deal of indecision when difficult choices had to be made.

Cromwell was the first to admit that he was no intellectual, having 'as little skill in Arithmetic as I have in the Law'.[2] He certainly was no political thinker and read few books besides the Bible, but he knew both the Old and New Testaments inside out and could quote them by heart. It was this devotion to the Bible that helps to make Cromwell's thinking more transparent. In many ways, Cromwell seemed to view scripture as a set of 'templates' around which to rationalize his own experiences. In the ever shifting and uncertain circumstances through which he lived it probably fortified him to draw parallels with more familiar paradigms. Unlike the clear-cut signs of divine favour through victory on the battlefields of the Civil War, it was much tougher to discern which path to take once the fighting was over. The Bible thus helped Cromwell when at his most indecisive to come to extremely difficult conclusions. The many speeches he gave to Parliament often have the feeling of sermons rather than political orations, littered as they are with biblical references. If it was the mind that made the man, it was the Bible that made Cromwell's mind tick.

Of course Cromwell's Biblicism was not the sole factor informing the way he made decisions. It was complemented by his notorious bouts of soul searching, during which he would attempt to read God's hidden 'providences' in the events around him. It also ran contrary to his conservative instinct, at times a limiting factor on his actions but often taking second place to what he believed to be God's will. By understanding how Cromwell both thought and expressed himself, we can start to explore more clearly how he came to some of the most important decisions in his political career. In particular, it helps to explain both why he became so committed to regicide in 1649, and so vehemently opposed to accepting the offer of the Crown in 1657. Ultimately, by examining Cromwell's thinking, that is his mind, we can get closer to the man himself.

*   *   *

What if a man should take upon him to be king?[3]
Oliver Cromwell, November 1652

If there is one question to sum up the political dilemma facing Cromwell from 1647 through to his death in 1658, it was surely this one. This one line, worthy of Macbeth and so often taken as evidence of Cromwell's self-seeking desire to seize the Crown for himself, might not be quite as simple as it seems. Admittedly, his interlocutor at the time, the lawyer Bulstrode Whitelocke, himself believed this to be further evidence of Cromwell's 'ambitious designs'. But the original question is ambivalent; it is what if 'a man', any man, should be king, not necessarily Cromwell. Behind it lurked a number of other issues. Was monarchy still valid as a form of government? Was rule by a single person justified? Who should decide what form of constitutional settlement was legitimate? Following three years of 'republican' government by a single-chamber parliament, Cromwell's question in 1652 was as much about his frustration with oligarchic rule by a group of self-serving MPs, than it was a recommendation of monarchy. Yet the problem it hit upon was a universal one. Its resonance was just as important in 1649 when the future of monarchy still hung in the balance, as it would be in 1657 when Cromwell himself turned down the Crown.

It was also a question that would have been unthinkable for Oliver in 1647. With the Royalist forces vanquished, settlement was to be achieved by Parliament through a negotiated treaty with, not without, the king. The *form* of government was not open to discussion, all that was required were a few constitutional safeguards to restrain the way the king exercised his power. Regicide and the abolition of monarchy were an unimaginable outcome. Cromwell did not move easily into the actions that would see his body punished as a 'traitor' at the

Restoration. Yet, within the space of just two years, attitudes shifted markedly. Men change their minds; nowhere is this clearer than in the case of Oliver Cromwell.

* * *

It is hard to feel sympathy for Charles I. Scheming, duplicitous, over-confident and oblivious to political realities, one cannot imagine a king more suited for bringing his three kingdoms to the brink of civil war. His unbending authoritarianism twinned with high-handed innovations in religion and taxation alienated a sufficient proportion of his subjects to provoke them into open rebellion. It was these less than endearing qualities that would be his ultimate undoing. Even in defeat, Charles was far from magnanimous. The fatal combination of an uncompromising nature and a total dearth of political astuteness made Charles I a very tough person with which to negotiate. He was a total roadblock to a viable settlement, prevaricating over even the most reasonable peace terms while secretly trying to broker deals with Parliament's enemies in order to plunge the nation into yet more bloodshed.

Just one example of his deviousness was his decision to surrender to the Scottish army at Newark in May 1646. With the Royalist cause staring at certain defeat, Charles slipped out of his besieged headquarters at Oxford and fled north in disguise. His intentions were clear enough; he hoped to start a bidding war over peace terms between the Scots and their English Parliamentarian allies. Yet Charles was not really interested in negotiating treaties. Lurking behind his professions of peace was a more sinister motive, namely a desire to turn the Scots against their Parliamentarian allies in his favour. In this instance the plan did not work and by February 1647 Charles was handed over into English custody. Charles I's strategy, however, would change little in the period from 1646 to 1649. Fortified by a belief that no settlement could be achieved without his assent, he procrastinated and haggled over terms in the hope that he could exploit the tensions and disagreements between those he negotiated with and provoke them into a new war.

Parliament for its part had more than just the king to deal with now that hostilities were over. The Civil War had been costly in both human lives and heavy taxation. With the Royalist threat subdued, there was a growing feeling in Parliament, especially among the so-called conservative 'Presbyterian' MPs, that it was time to disband Parliament's forces, including the New Model Army, thereby reducing the burden on the counties. The way in which this was handled, however, lacked sensitivity for the material grievances of the army. Already owed around three million pounds in pay, the soldiery were unwilling to disband before they could be certain that they would see the money owed to them. An atmosphere of mutual mistrust began to develop between Parliament and its army. Petitions were drafted among the rank and file demanding sufficient monetary and legal guarantees before they returned to civilian life. The response of the Presbyterians in the Commons, led by Denzil Holles, was a suicidal vote on 30 March 1647 that warned that all those who continued to petition would be looked upon as 'enemies of the state and disturbers of the public peace'.

It was a profound statement for Parliament to make against its own forces. The New Model Army had prided itself on its honour and did not take too kindly to these slurs. This was the spark that fired the army into political action. As the Parliament persisted with plans for the army's disbandment, the army deepened its resolve not to put down its arms until its grievances were satisfied. A 'General Council' of the army, consisting of the general officers of the army (including Cromwell and Ireton), joined by two commissioned officers and two representatives of the soldiery (known as 'agitators') from each regiment, was established in June to co-ordinate the achievement of these goals. This General Council both legitimized and neutered the agitation among the rank and file by bringing them back under the firm supervision of the general officers of the army. Officers and common soldiers now stood united in their opposition to Parliament's actions.

Indeed, the army claimed not only to act in its own interests, but also in the interests of the nation as a whole against the tyranny of the Presbyterian majority in Parliament. In the *Declaration of the Army* of 14 June, an army 'mission statement' drawn up by Commissary-General Henry Ireton, the army asserted its right to speak in the name of all 'free-born people of England', stating 'We were not a mere mercenary army hired to serve an arbitrary power of a state, but called forth and conjured by the several declarations of parliament to the defence of our own the people's just rights and liberties'. In order to bring this about, Parliament would not just need purging of Holles and his friends, but reforming wholesale. The present Parliament would be dissolved and a perpetual succession of fixed-term Parliaments would follow. Constituencies should be reapportioned to get rid of rotten boroughs and make Parliament more 'representative of the whole'.

To bring about its vision, however, the army would need a bargaining tool. On 4 June 1647, they were provided with one after a daring move to seize King Charles I from Parliamentary imprisonment. Fears had begun to grow over a possible Presbyterian plot to bring the king to London in order to broker a deal to the detriment of the army. Cornet George Joyce, holding the lowest commissioned rank in Sir Thomas Fairfax's regiment of horse, set out with a force of 500 and a mandate, possibly from Cromwell personally, to secure the king's person at Holmby House and prevent any attempts to remove him. Yet at some point Joyce lost his nerve. Although he had secured Charles by the evening of 3 June, and replaced the garrison there with his own men, he began to fear reports of nearby pro-Presbyterian forces. By late evening he had resolved to move the king to a more secure location. When Charles I rode out of Holmby the next morning, the flimsiness of Joyce's authority was revealed. Charles, unruffled by his rude awakening, merely inquired, 'What commission have you to secure my person?' Joyce's initial silence was deafening. Sensing the cornet's discomfort, Charles continued to press the point: 'Have you nothing in writing from Sir Thomas Fairfax, your general, to do what you do?' Joyce's infamous reply was a mere gesticulation towards the ranks of cavalrymen behind him: 'It is behind me'. Charles understood the situation all too well: 'It is as fair a commission and as well written as I have seen a commission written in my life: a company of handsome, proper gentlemen as I have seen a great while'.[4]

Despite the sabre-rattling, Charles I could hardly be described as acting under duress. Joyce, lacking any sort of plan, sought Charles's opinion on where he should be moved. It was the king personally who asked to be taken to army headquarters at Newmarket. Perceiving the chance to cause more trouble for those with whom he was supposed to be negotiating, Charles all too willingly set off to meet the army's top brass. Although at first Fairfax would berate Joyce's actions, he came to accede to the king's wishes. All this placed the army officers, notably Lieutenant-General Oliver Cromwell and Commissary-General Henry Ireton, in a very dubious position. With possession of the king, they were now the main brokers of any possible peace settlement between Charles and his Parliament. The summer of 1647 was punctuated by both threats and use of force against the Parliament, causing the withdrawal of 11 of the leading Presbyterian MPs (including Denzil Holles) who had been the ringleaders behind the disbandment scheme of the spring. At the same time, the army officers began to sit around the negotiating table with Charles in order to work out the future settlement for the nation.

The document around which the army's negotiations were centred, entitled *The Heads of Proposals*, was initially drafted by Ireton and a group of influential peers before coming under discussion at the General Council of the army in mid-July 1647. Compared to the peace terms offered to Charles under Scottish captivity at Newcastle in 1646, these army proposals were relatively mild. Very few of Charles's supporters were exempted from a general pardon and Charles, unlike the Scottish proposals, was not obliged to abolish bishops and bring in a Presbyterian form of church government. There was to be no major change in the political fabric: the king would be given much the same role as before, albeit with some safeguards regarding the calling and meeting of Parliaments.

Yet, even on such generous terms, Charles remained obstinate. When the *Heads* were formerly presented to him on 28 July at Woburn, his response betrayed his usually cool equivocating manner. He was adamant that not one of his supporters should be punished for their actions in the Civil War and went on to deliver a strong rebuke to the assembled officers: 'You cannot do without me! You will fall to ruin if I do not sustain you'. A shocked silence must have filled the room as the officers discovered just how uncompromising their captive would be. Equally aghast was Charles's confidant and intermediary Sir John Berkeley, who, taking Charles aside, whispered words of caution: 'Sir, your Majesty speaks as if you had some secret strength and power that I do not know of; and since you Majesty hath concealed it from me, I wish you had concealed it from these men also'.[5] Remarkably, despite continued stonewalling from Charles, the army officers persisted with their negotiations into the autumn. Charles returned to his usual practice of supplying 'half-answers' to the proposals put to him, which failed either to endorse or refute what he was offered. Even now, very few men could seriously contemplate a settlement without the king. When, for example, Henry Marten put forward a motion in the Commons in September to stop further negotiations with the king, Oliver Cromwell acted as the 'teller' of the votes against Marten. The inherent conservatism within Cromwell still held sway over his reason. The events of the next few months, however, would start to see the development of a very different, even uncomfortable, way of thinking about monarchy.

* * *

The continued, prolonged and fruitless negotiations between the army officers and Charles started to take their
toll on the soldiery as a whole. Rumours and suspicions
began to abound over the motives of Cromwell and Ireton in their clandestine meetings with the king. These
army 'grandees', as they became sneeringly known, were
believed to be cutting themselves a lucrative deal with the
king while ignoring the original reason the army had
taken to its rebellion: the plight of the soldiers. The
Heads of the Proposals was criticized by the soldiery because
it seemed to subordinate the army's grievances and the
rights of the people to those of the king. As one critic later
remarked, the *Heads* would merely bring the nation back
to square one, under the same oppressions as before the
wars began: 'they shall but sow the wind and reap the
whirlwind... I know no other use of those Proposals than
to support the tottering reputation of the grand officers
in the minds of such as shall not discern their vanity'.[6]

By autumn 1647 this sense of betrayal at the hands of
the grandees was rife. On 15 October these grievances
were printed in a strident document entitled *The Case of
the Army Truly Stated*. Although purporting to be the
work of the Agitators or 'Agents' of five regiments, it was
actually the product of a group of London radicals known
as the Levellers, who were hoping to give their political
ideas a platform among the soldiery. Claiming to speak
for the whole army and addressed to the commander of
the Parliamentarian forces, Sir Thomas Fairfax, the *Case*

drew on the groundswell of mistrust against the grandees. It delivered a stinging rebuke against the army officers, especially Ireton and Cromwell, for straying from the demands and declarations originally made by the army in the spring of 1647. Because these men had grown so obsessed with negotiating with Charles on any terms, it had led to 'a total neglect of insisting positively upon the redress of those grievances, or granting those desires of the Army as Soldiers ... the peoples expectations that were much greatened, and their hopes of relief in their miseries and oppressions which were so much heightened are like to be frustrated'.[7]

This was a bitter pill for Cromwell to swallow. Such grievous charges needed to be quashed, and it was decided to use the now weekly meetings of the General Council of the Army as a forum in which to do this. The so-called 'Putney Debates', which lasted from 28 October through to mid-November 1647, now celebrated for Colonel Thomas Rainsborough's impassioned outburst that, 'the poorest hee that is in England hath a life to live as the greatest hee', were actually convened in order to defend the grandee's negotiations with the king. Cromwell was in the Chair of the Council for the duration due to the poor health of Lord General Fairfax. Throughout the debates we see Oliver listening intently, trying desperately to guide debate, as well as providing support to Ireton's vehement defence of the political status quo. The language was stormy. Those who had been behind the

Case of the Army did not mince their words. Confronting the grandees face to face in the confined space of Putney Church, Trooper Edward Sexby was not afraid to criticize his superiors: 'Wee have labour'd to please a Kinge, and I thinke, except wee goe about to cutt all our throates, wee shall nott please him'. Addressing Cromwell and Ireton, Sexby exclaimed that 'your creditts and reputation hath bin much blasted' by their fruitless negotiations with the king.

It must have been a disturbing experience for Cromwell. So long loved by the army for his brilliant leadership on the battlefield, he began to see the difficulties that came with peace. Cromwell was probably not as concerned about his own dwindling popularity than he was with the self-destructive impact such bickering would have on both army discipline and finding a viable means of settling the nation. The unity of purpose that the army demonstrated in the heat of battle had now melted away. With the acrimony of debate escalating, an expedient was suggested to try and help bring about consensus—they would seek God. All those present at the General Council were invited to a prayer meeting the following morning before the resumption of debates. For Cromwell, such a meeting was extremely necessary: 'I thinke itt will bee requisite that wee doe itt speedily, and doe itt the first thinge, and that wee doe itt as unitedly as wee can… For my parte I shall lay aside all businesse for this businesse, either to convince or bee convinc't as God shall please'. Such tactics might, at first, seem like a cynical attempt to time-waste and throw debate off course. Yet, these prayer meetings were a consistent and frequent part of Cromwell's decision-making process. Many of the most important events in Cromwell's political career came after seeking God's pleasure in the company of a few close confidants. They were effectively divine sounding boards leading him into action—not always in the direction of his instincts.

Men were encouraged to turn up to these meetings with a free mind. Moments of silent contemplation were punctuated by sudden outbursts from those assembled. A passage from the Bible would be quoted that seemed particularly apposite to the situation or problem being pondered upon. For the meeting of the 29 October, we do not have a full record and do not know whether Cromwell floated any of his own scriptural musings. Lieutentant-Colonel William Goffe's meditations from that morning, however, do survive. His subject was the Book of Revelations, the conclusions he reached somewhat alarming for conservative men. Goffe demonstrated how the kings of England had overthrown the Antichristian power of the Pope, only to claim that power themselves. 'Lett us inquire', he exclaimed, 'whether some of the actions that wee have done of late, some of the thinges that wee have propounded of late, doe nott crosse the worke of God ... because in our proposing of thinges we doe indeavour to sett uppe that power that God would nott sett uppe againe'. This was a clear rebuke against those who had been so willing to set Charles back on his throne at any cost. The force of his words was somewhat tempered by a later reading from the Book of Numbers which counselled caution: 'Let us nott now in a kinde of heate run uppe and say, "wee will goe now:" because itt may bee there is a better opportunity that God will give us'. Yet, the kernel of his argument would continue to have a resonance throughout the next 15 months.

Rather than foster union, the prayer meeting further exposed their divisions. It also had a profound effect on Cromwell—not quite an epiphany, but it certainly set his mind in motion. With Goffe's words ringing in his ears, he began to extend his exegesis to its logical conclusion, that is, he thought the unthinkable. On 1 November 1647, Cromwell, still in the Chair of the General Council, tried his best to continue his defence of the political fabric, but markedly shifted emphasis. Uncomfortable suggestions were made concerning the king's future, including Sexby's exhortation that, 'we find in the worde of God: "I would heal Babylon but shee would not be healed." I think that wee have gone about to heale Babylon when shee would not'. More striking was Captain George Bishop's reading of God's will: 'After many inquiries in my spirit I find this answer … I say [it is] a compliance to preserve that Man of Blood, and those principles of tyranny which God from Heaven by his many successes has manifestly declared against, and which I am confident may be our destruction'.

Such words Cromwell could not allow to pass lightly. Yet his response was not as firm as many might have expected. 'We all apprehend danger from the person of the King', was his frank answer. More profoundly he went on to admit how it was his own belief that 'there can bee no safety in a consistency with the person of the King'. Yet, even if, as he admitted, 'forms of government are dross and dung in comparison to Christ', the problem of a bad king was not enough to bring the whole political edifice tumbling down. His advice was to wait and see where God would take them: 'Let those that are of that mind [i.e. to remove Charles] wait upon God for such a way when the thing may be done without sin and without scandal too'. Cromwell was not advocating regicide in November 1647, but neither was he ruling it out.[8]

* * *

Charles I's next actions helped to make Cromwell's decision a little easier. On 12 November 1647, Charles fled from his captivity at Hampton Court to the Isle of Wight. While the army was busy bickering, Charles had been in secret negotiations with a party in Scotland, led by his cousin, the Duke of Hamilton. By December, he had signed an 'Engagement' with these Scottish allies that would bring fresh conflict into England.

The effect this had on both the army in general and Cromwell in particular was immense. With the threat of another war, the divisions in the army evaporated. The news of Scottish preparations for an invasion of England, coupled with numerous local risings, most notably in South Wales, provoked the army to seek God once more. Meeting at Windsor in April 1648, the army met to reflect on scriptural testimony and seek the answer to their present conundrum. Cromwell urged those present to consider 'our actions as an Army, as well as our ways particularly, as private Christians, to see if any iniquity could be found in them'. They sought to find the route of their problems, 'and so remove the cause of such sad rebukes' as they had faced in recent months. Unlike Putney, there was now no spirit of temperance evident. Once again, William Goffe took the lead, using the Book of Proverbs as his guide and its key phrase: 'Turn you at my reproof'. The impact was immense. According to one then present, Goffe's words:

begot in us a great sense, shame, and loathing our selves for our iniquities, and justifying the Lord as righteous in his proceedings against us: and in this path the Lord led us not only to see our sin, but also our duty; and this so unanimously set with weight upon each heart, that none was able hardly to speak a word to each other for bitter weeping.

Goffe's meaning was obvious to all present. Charles I was the source of their 'iniquity'. The grandee's misplaced trust in the king had provoked God's rebuke in the form of a Second Civil War. In order to make amends the army had to reverse this policy, they had to 'turn at His reproof'.[9]

Without dissent the assembled officers agreed it was their duty to go and fight their 'potent enemies', but moreover it was also necessary to bring the king to justice for what he had done. That is: 'If ever the Lord brought us back again in peace, to call *Charles Stuart*, that man of blood, to an account, for that blood he had shed, mischief he had done, to his utmost, against the Lord's cause and people in these poor Nations'. What had been the demand of a minority within the army just six months earlier had now become mainstream.

The effects this meeting at Windsor had on Cromwell must have been profound. At Putney, Cromwell had counselled caution to those claiming to act in the name of God for fear that they may be reading too much into His Providences. At Windsor, however, the unitary voice with which the army officers spoke acted as a potent convincer for Oliver. The signs and warnings from God, backed up by biblical references, had by now become so glaringly obvious to Cromwell and the other grandees that it was no longer necessary to question the divine path along which they were being taken. The series of crushing defeats that Cromwell inflicted on Royalist forces during this Second Civil War, most notably at Preston, further entrenched this sense of God's purpose. For Cromwell, those who had provoked this new war were below contempt: 'Their fault who have appeared in this summer's business is certainly double to theirs who were in the first, because it is the repetition of the same offence against all the witnesses that God has borne, by making and abetting to a second war'.[10] To cross God once was bad enough, to cross Him twice was unforgivable.

While the army was growing increasingly sure of the need to remove Charles, Parliament frantically sought to broker a hasty peace with him on the Isle of Wight. Yet, even with his forces facing certain defeat, Charles would make no concessions. Desperately, the conservative MPs who attended him tried to get Charles to accept terms, twice extending the 'deadline' of the negotiations in the hope that the king would change his mind. All this was the final straw for the army grandees. Once more, Henry Ireton took a key role in drafting a new army manifesto. This *Remonstrance* of the army, however, would display none of the conservatism of the *Heads* of just a year before. Presented to the army's council at St Albans on 18 November, it unambiguously laid out a plan to purge Parliament of those who had tried to cut a deal with Charles and, more importantly, ordered the king's trial. Its chief aim was to ensure that Charles Stuart, 'the capital and grand author of all our troubles', would at last be brought to justice. Charles's duplicitous nature had finally become his undoing.

* * *

Cromwell's role in the events of late 1648 is slightly perplexing. Although clearly committed to bringing the king to justice while embroiled in the crucible of war, in the calm of peace he seemed momentarily to get cold feet. Rather than joining Ireton and the other army grandees in London, he remained in the north, at Pontefract, mopping up the few outposts of resistance that still held out. A vivid insight into his thinking at this point is provided by his correspondence to his cousin Robert Hammond, then in charge of the garrison guarding the king on the Isle of Wight. Within these letters we find Cromwell attempting to convince Hammond of the necessity of bringing the king to trial. Yet, at the same time, there is also a hint that Cromwell was trying to think out matters for his own peace of mind.

These letters are crammed full of biblical references and providential examples, indicating just how much Cromwell felt his words needed justification. Writing on 25 November 1648, clearly aware of the army's growing resolve in London as a result of the publication of the *Remonstrance*, Cromwell implored Hammond to 'look into providences; surely they mean somewhat. They hang so together; have been so constant, so clear and unclouded'. All the signs—the Royalist defeat; Charles's unwillingness to accept even the most reasonable peace terms; the growing frustration in the army—were indicators of God's design. In a complete *volte face* to his words of prudence at Putney, Cromwell now threw caution to the wind. The army's actions were not 'a tempting of God', for: 'tempting of God ordinarily is either by acting presumptuously in carnal confidence, or in unbelief through diffidence: both these ways Israel tempted God in the wilderness, and He was grieved by them'. The army's intentions, however, were pure as they were done out of faith alone, not from 'fleshly reasoning'. Providence had disposed 'the hearts of so many of God's people this way, especially in this poor Army, wherein the great God has vouchsafed to appear'. So many men couldn't be wrong, without doubt Charles I was 'this Man, against whom the Lord hath witnessed'.[11]

Yet Cromwell's words did not match his actions. He continued to dither in the north while events in London took hold. Despite demands from Fairfax to come south with all speed on 28 November, it took over a week for Cromwell to reach the capital—almost double the time expected for such a journey. While Henry Ireton was co-ordinating arrangements to purge the Commons of those MPs who had continued to demand a treaty with Charles, Cromwell was slowly marching southwards. By the time Cromwell arrived in London, on the evening of 6 December, the infamous 'Pride's Purge' had already been committed. According to the hostile commentary of the Republican Edmund Ludlow, on arrival at Whitehall Cromwell declared, 'that he had not been acquainted with this design; yet since it was done, he was glad of it, and would endeavour to maintain it'.[12] That Cromwell knew nothing is highly unlikely given his regular corre-spondence with the army officers in London. What this episode does reveal, however, is that for all the godly fervour Cromwell displayed throughout 1648, his mind was never completely free from its conservative restraints. When difficult and legally dubious matters came to a head, such as purging Parliament and executing the king, Cromwell preferred to lurk in the shadows while others took the lead.

Indeed, even while the purged Parliament began its preparations for the trial, there is evidence to suggest that Cromwell was still seeking a compromise. Although utterly convinced of Charles I's inability to rule, Cromwell is reputed to have been behind a mission to send the Earl of Denbigh to obtain Charles's abdication in favour of one of his sons. Thus initially Cromwell sought to replace rather than kill the king.[13] Perhaps Cromwell realized that there were too many men, like his cousin Hammond, who failed to buy into the notion of a divinely appointed regicide to ever make king-killing a 'popular' act. It was a matter of political pragmatism; to avoid alienating most of English society, and to make the army's recent coup more palatable, Cromwell hoped to keep Charles alive. Unsurprisingly, Charles would have none of it and preparations for his trial continued apace.

Finally convinced that both Providence and necessity demanded the execution of the king, Oliver took to his task with alacrity. On 6 January 1649, Parliament passed an Act appointing 135 commissioners, including Cromwell and Ireton, to a High Court of Justice to try Charles I. The court was presided over by their fellow traveller at

Tyburn, John Bradshaw. That the Commons had to rely on this relatively low-ranking, obscure lawyer to guide the trial is indicative of the revulsion with which most of the legal profession viewed the proceedings. Yet, while some commissioners left the capital, an important minority remained firm. Cromwell attended every day of the trial, which began on 20 January 1649 in Westminster Hall, and his name can be seen in the trial papers held in the National Archives (see plates 8 and 9). The charge against the king was a weighty one: 'the said Charles Stuart hath been, and is the occasioner, author, and continuer of the said unnatural, cruel and bloody wars; and therein guilty of all the treasons, murders, rapines, burnings, spoils, desolations, damages and mischiefs to this nation, acted and committed in the said wars, or occasioned thereby'.[14]

Charles, to the bitter end, refused to answer this charge. No longer displaying his characteristic stutter, Charles spoke confidently and defiantly. 'I would know by what power I am called hither... I would know by what authority, I mean *lawful* authority... Remember I am your King, your *lawful* King... I have a trust committed to me by God, by old and lawful descent' was his terse reply (see plate 10). Bradshaw, clearly rattled by Charles's composed answer, retorted that Charles was called to trial 'by the authority of the Commons of England ... on the behalf of the people of England by which you are elected king'. Charles must have smiled to himself as he set Bradshaw straight on the nation's constitutional history:

> England was never an Elective Kingdom, it was a Heredi-
> tary Kingdom for near this thousand years. Therefore
> let me know by what authority I am called hither. Your
> authority [is] raised by an usurped power ... I will never
> betray my trust, I am entrusted with the liberty of my
> people, I doe stand more for the liberties of my people
> then any one that is seated here as a judge.

The trial proved a farcical stalemate with Charles consis-
tently refusing to answer the charges against him while
pouring scorn on those who claimed a right to try him.
The result was inevitable. Cromwell was the third of fifty-
nine people to sign the king's death warrant on 29 January 1649; the execution followed the next day.[15]

The gruesome 'executions' of Cromwell, Ireton and
Bradshaw at Tyburn, 12 years later, were supposed to
erase the memory of regicide. Their heads placed over the
south end of Westminster Hall, above the very location in
which they had sat in judgement over the king. Yet, one
must question how much Cromwell really was to blame
for the downfall of Charles I. Undoubtedly, the character
of the king himself was a major factor. The deep sense of
mistrust that he created through his underhand dealings,
duplicitous negotiations and stubborn refusal to compromise meant that he had become too dangerous a man
with which to build a lasting settlement. It became

simpler to remove him than to persist any longer—a 'cruel necessity'.

Despite this, however, Cromwell's backing for regicide was not a decision made lightly. It grated against his inherent conservative outlook and perhaps led him to persist with alternative solutions for longer than others such as Ireton. Driving him forward was godly reasoning. With the Bible as his guide, he began to see the scriptural parallels with his own plight. Yet these thoughts alone were not enough. They were fortified by a reading of God's Providence in the events through which he was being propelled. Not just in text, but in actions also, God was providing signs to help the army officers reach their difficult conclusions.

Moreover, one should not underestimate the effect others, especially in the army, had on Cromwell. The intense spiritual cauldron of the army's prayer meetings acted as a catalyst, setting in motion many of the decisions reached by Cromwell. He was never completely beholden to follow the advice or opinions of others, but he did like to know the minds of other men in order to test his own conclusions.

The Bible, Providence, the army and an inherent, lingering conservatism were all factors that affected the way Cromwell thought about important political decisions. Just as they had a significant bearing on his decision to execute the king, so they would also come to bear on an equally difficult matter: the offer of the Crown.

* * *

It might, at first, seem ironic, even comical, that a man who had helped to see one king executed would eventually himself be offered the Crown. That the offer was made in the first place was borne out of frustration. Since the king's death in 1649, followed by the abolition of monarchy and the House of Lords, no one stable government had been settled. The kingless 'Commonwealth' ruled over by the 'Rump' Parliament (created by the army's purge in December 1648) proved self-serving and had an uncanny ability to rub the army up the wrong way. Following its stormy dissolution in April 1653 at the hands of Cromwell, a short-lived experiment followed whereby a 'nominated assembly' of godly persons was entrusted with the task of providing for future settlement. When this fell through in December 1653, power was returned to the army and its commander in chief, Cromwell. Within days Cromwell was invested as 'Lord Protector' under a military-backed constitution entitled *The Instrument of Government*, drafted by Major-General John Lambert. When Parliament met under this new constitution, in September 1654, the reception was frosty. MPs questioned what right the army had to impose such a document; only Parliament had the power to create a constitution. Despite Cromwell's pleas to accept the new constitutional arrangements, Parliament proved unresponsive and was dissolved in January 1655, leaving the legality of Oliver's powers in serious doubt.

The offer of the Crown to Cromwell in 1657 was part of a constitutional package designed to replace the *Instrument*. The men behind this offer were conservative, 'civilian' supporters of Cromwell who had grown tired of the unstable nature of the Interregnum government and abhorred the undue influence of the army. Unlike the *Instrument*, this *Humble Petition and Advice* was offered by Parliament thus removing any doubts over legitimacy. It was designed to rebuild the political fabric destroyed so abruptly in 1649. Its first article emphatically stated: 'That your Highness will be pleased to assume, the name, style, title, dignity, & office of king of England, Scotland & Ireland and the respective dominions & territories there unto belonging and to exercise the same according to the laws of these nations'.[16]

Moreover, Parliaments were to consist of two chambers again, with a nominated 'Other House' of 70 members to take the place of the House of Lords. If Cromwell had accepted this document the result would have been the restoration of monarchy under the rule of King Oliver I.

This was both the easiest and most difficult decision that Cromwell would have to make. His conservative instincts must have momentarily clouded his decision. He allegedly berated a meeting of army officers in late February 1657 for complaining about Parliament's offer. Not only did he liken the title of king to a mere 'feather in a hat', a title signifying very little, he also made a very telling admission: 'It is time to come to a settlement, and lay aside arbitrary proceedings, so unacceptable to the nation'.[17] The last four years of political experimentation had only helped to alienate the majority of the nation against novel forms of government backed by military force. They needed to return to known ways, for 'healing and settling' as Cromwell termed it. Overjoyed by Cromwell's rebuke against these whinging army officers, those MPs who had drafted the *Humble Petition* must have been confident that Cromwell was going to give his full assent. Indeed, before the document was given to Oliver, Parliament even added the proviso that if he failed to agree to *all* the clauses in the *Humble Petition* 'then nothing in the same be deemed of force'.[18] In short, the terms of the new constitution were non-negotiable: it was kingship or bust.

To the consternation of Parliament, however, Cromwell's answer was by no means clear-cut. When the *Humble Petition* was presented to him on 31 March 1657 he gave a very evasive answer. The matter was 'a thing of weight; the greatest weight of anything that ever was laid upon a man'. The way he sought to resolve this problem was by now a familiar one: 'I have been many times at a loss, which way to stand under the weight of what hath laid upon me: – but by looking at the conduct and pleasure of God in it. Which hitherto I have found to be a good pleasure towards me'.[19] He asked for a short time for 'the utmost deliberation and consideration' on this matter before he gave his answer. On 3 April 1657, after days of seeking God coupled with bouts of ill health, he made his reply. Although he praised the document for its care to preserve both religious and civil liberties, there was one major stumbling block:

> You do necessitate my answer to be categorical; and you have left me without a liberty of choice as to all … seeing the way is hedged up so as it is to me, I cannot accept the things offered unless I accept all, I have not been able to find it my duty to God and you to undertake this charge under that Title [of King]… Nothing must make a man's conscience a servant.[20]

Although shaken by this sudden blow, the conservatives in Parliament remained adamant that Cromwell should take the Crown and refused to take 'no' for an answer. In the series of meetings that took place over the following month between Cromwell and a specially appointed 'committee of 99' MPs, one can really start to see Oliver's mind in motion. Just as in 1649, his ultimate conclusions were reached through a combination of scriptural interpretation, providential thinking and army influence.

Throughout April, this committee of 99 tried to get Oliver to change his mind. In particular, a number of prominent lawyers endeavoured to appeal to Cromwell's conservative side. Typical of their arguments, was that of Master of the Rolls, William Lenthall, who chastened Cromwell for believing that kingship was nothing more than a 'Title':

It carries more in it of weight than a mere *Title*; for upon due consideration you shall find that the whole body of the Law is carried upon this Wheel, it is not a thing that stands on the top merely, but runs through the whole life and veins of the Law.[21]

Moreover, the 'title' of king was also a known quantity. Everybody knew the powers and limitations of a king, whereas, as Sir Charles Wolseley argued, 'the law knows not a Lord Protector'.[22]

This was not enough to convince Oliver. He freely admitted to them that 'your arguments, which I say were chiefly upon the Law, seem to carry with them a great deal of necessary conclusiveness, to enforce that one thing of Kingship'.[23] But, at the same time there was 'nothing of necessity' in their argument. It was not enough to argue that the whole body of law was carried on this title as 'The Supreme Authority going in another Name and under another Title than that of King, why it hath been already complied with twice without it'. That is, the Commonwealth government after Charles I's death and, more recently, Cromwell's Protectorate had both survived without that title. The courts still functioned, taxes were still paid, and life went on.

For Cromwell, there were more weighty reasons on his mind that simply meant he could never countenance taking the Crown. Once again, his conservative scruples would give way to his spiritual zeal. His reasoning was revealed most vividly in a speech to the Parliamentary committee on 13 April 1657:

> Truly the Providence of God hath laid aside this Title of King providentially de facto: and this not by sudden humour or passion… It hath been the issue of Ten or Twelve Years Civil War, wherein much blood hath been shed… And God hath seemed Providentially… not only to strike at the Family but at the Name… God hath seemed so to deal with the Persons and the Family that He blasted the very Title… I will not seek to set up that, that Providence hath destroyed, and laid in the dust; and I would not build Jericho again![24]

God had sanctioned the abolition of monarchy; to set up kingship again would be to fly in the face of divine will. Cromwell's conclusions had a scriptural basis. The reference to Jericho betrays Cromwell's fear of repeating the 'sin of Achan' described in the Book of Joshua. After the destruction of Jericho, Achan had coveted and pillaged treasure including 'the accursed thing'. As a result the Israelites as a whole were punished—God withheld any further victories from Joshua and his armies. Only when Achan's sin was discovered and he was stoned and burned to death would God's anger be sated. For Cromwell, the parallel was exact. He should not take upon himself the 'accursed thing' and thereby bring divine wrath upon the nation—he should not rebuild Jericho. In many ways, his thinking was no different to that of William Goffe at

Putney almost a decade before: they should not resurrect that which 'God would not set up again'.

Cromwell did not refuse the Crown because he feared his colleagues in the army would prevent him from taking it. His stern rebuttal to the meeting of army officers in late February was evidence of that. Their opinions, however, did count for a lot. He valued highly the thoughts of those who had seen the direct workings of God's Providences on the battlefields of the Civil War. Typical of the feeling in the army at the time was a letter from a former soldier of the New Model Army named William Bradford. He was one who had fought with Cromwell in all the major battles from 'Edghill to Dunbar' and had great respect for his commander: 'when we were in our lowest condition, your tears and prayers much satisfied many'. He counselled Cromwell not to now turn his back on his former godly allies by taking the Crown, warning him menacingly to 'remember you are a man, and must die, and come to judgement'.[25] This put a heavy burden of spiritual pressure on the Lord Protector's shoulders, but it also fortified him. This process was no different to the army prayer meetings of 1647–8. Cromwell was listening intently to other people's reading of God's word, their own interpretations of Providence. Even if he did not feel obliged to follow their advice, he liked to sound them out in order to be sure of his own 'interpretation' of God's purpose. In this case, like in 1649, both Cromwell and his army were as one in their thoughts.

On 8 May Oliver Cromwell's final answer was to come in an uncharacteristically short and overtly apologetic speech to Parliament:

> Although I think the Act of Government doth consist of very excellent parts, in all but in that one thing of the Title … I say I am persuaded to return this Answer to you, That I cannot undertake this Government with that Title of King. And that is mine Answer to this great and weighty Business.

Many of the MPs who had invested so much effort in the *Humble Petition* walked out in disgust. Some remained and thrashed out a 'deal' by which Cromwell would adopt the *Humble Petition* but under his old title of Lord Protector. The expedient passed the House by just three votes on 22 May and Cromwell gave his assent a few days later. This was the outcome Cromwell had hoped for all along—he gained the benefits of a Parliamentary constitution without the burden of kingship.

Although Cromwell's inauguration ceremony as Lord Protector under this new constitution had all the trappings of a royal coronation, it conspicuously lacked a crown. Despite Cromwell spending the final few years of his life living in 'royal' palaces and conferring 'royal' gifts, including two hereditary baronages, his own thoughts remained distinctly un-royal. Throughout the Protectorate, Cromwell preferred to liken himself to Moses: leading the people of Israel (the English) from Egyptian captivity (the tyranny of Charles I) and through the wilderness to the Promised Land. But, at the same time, he also had a more humble wish influenced by the story of Gideon in the book of Judges. Gideon was a lowly farmer who came to lead the armies of Israel and destroy the Midianites. With the Midianite kings executed, Gideon was offered the Crown but refused, preferring to retire to the tranquil anonymity of his farm. By the final year of his life Cromwell, frustrated by Parliament and feeling the heavy burden of his position, longed for a similar fate: 'I can say in the presence of God, in comparison of whom we are but like poor creeping ants upon the earth, I would have been glad to have lived under my woodside, to have kept a flock of sheep rather than undertook such a Government as this is'.[26]

The notion that Cromwell would have ever wanted to be a king is absurd. He was distinctly uncomfortable with the powers he did have and did not look to engross himself further. That Cromwell's funeral would see his crowned effigy paraded through London, owed more to the desperation of those who had failed to convince him to take the Crown in his lifetime, than to the desires of Oliver himself. The effigy was but a 'dead invented Image of Wood or Wax' as the Quaker Edward Burrough jeeringly described it.[27]

*   *   *

Cromwell's thinking was complex but not impenetrable. At those points where his mind was exercised on its toughest decisions, one can discern a familiar pattern. Cromwell was guided by his interpretation of both the Word and actions of God. Although displaying a conservative streak, it was God that drove him forward; who made him see that 'necessity' was as good a justification as law; that political forms could be changed if corrupt in the eyes of God. Cromwell may have begun as a reluctant regicide, but it was God who fortified him and pushed him on through a decade of kingless rule. That Cromwell's head would never wear the Crown, thereby remaining true to his reading of God's will, is proof alone that the mind most definitely made the man.

Yet his refusal of the Crown had a significant impact on the longevity of the government over which he presided. Those conservatives who reeled in shock at Cromwell's rejection of their proposals began to step away from involvement in the Protectoral regime. The army continued to exercise its influence over Oliver's government and thus the majority of conservative men remained alienated. Whereas the acceptance of kingship would have grounded Cromwell's government firmly in the law, his rejection of it meant that the Protectorate would continue to function in its vague and ambivalent way, helping to finally bring about its collapse at the hands of the military grandees after his death. Maybe if Cromwell had listened to his conservative side and taken the Crown, the Restoration of Stuart monarchy three years later would have been avoidable. A Cromwellian monarchy might have had a better chance of gaining the support of the country at large than the legally dubious, pseudo-military Protectorate. It could have provided sufficient constitutional stability to ensure that the Stuarts never returned, thus avoiding the gruesome events of 1661. Cromwell's refusal of the Crown was perhaps his greatest achievement, but also his biggest mistake.

* IV *
Warts and All?

HOW MUCH do we *really* know about the man behind the head? Who was the *real* Oliver Cromwell? So much bad press has clouded his reputation in the years since the Restoration that it is not easy to uncover an accurate picture of Cromwell in life. Oliver himself professed to live in a 'plain' style and dealt with people in the same forthright manner. It was while Cromwell sat for a portrait by Sir Peter Lely (see plate 11) that he allegedly gave his now legendary advice to the painter:

> Mr. Lely I desire you would use all your skill to paint my picture truly like me and not flatter me at all. But (pointing to his own face) remark all these roughness, pimples warts & everything as you see me. Otherwise I never will pay a farthing for it.[1]

In many ways, however, this image of Cromwell was just as 'false' as the demonic one created in the Restoration period. Oliver Cromwell was never simply the puritanical caricature that he has often been made out to be. In reality, his personality displayed a number of traits, not just plain and godly but also humorous, loving and playful. He had both a complex upbringing and a happy family life. Behind the supposedly 'transparent' image that Cromwell himself sought to portray, lies a much more complicated character.

Like his head in death, Oliver in life was subject to a number of dramatic changes in fortune. From years in obscurity to a prominent place in the public spotlight, Cromwell's tale was just as remarkable as the posthumous journey of his head. Likewise, when examining Cromwell's reputation, one needs to proceed with the same meticulous eye to detail as the cranial detectives who examined Oliver's head in the early twentieth century. Only by seeing through the veneer of 300 years of legend can one truly understand Oliver in his own lifetime.

*   *   *

I was by birth a gentleman: living neither in any considerable height, nor yet in obscurity.
Oliver Cromwell to Parliament, 12 September 1654

Contrary to Cromwell's words, for the first 40 years of his life he was indeed an obscure figure. Like the fate of his head during the late seventeenth and early eighteenth centuries, one can catch a brief glimpse of Cromwell in the records now and again, but little more. In order to compensate for the paucity of the historical record, there has been much invented about Cromwell's early life. As with the story of his head, it provides a minefield of myths that should be treat with extreme caution.

Oliver Cromwell was born in Huntingdon, near Cambridge, on 25 April 1599, the only surviving son of Robert and Elizabeth Cromwell. His father was the younger son of a knight and a man of modest means, inheriting only a few urban properties around the town. Incredible tales and legends survive about Oliver's childhood, most of which are complete fabrications. Among the most far-fetched are claims that, as a baby, Cromwell was seized by a monkey that carried him through a window and dropped him from the rooftops where he all but met his death. Another romantic notion is that Oliver and Prince Charles played as toddlers when James I was visiting Cromwell's uncle, Sir Oliver, at Hinchingbrook House in the early 1600s. Cromwell and Charles got into a fight, so the story goes, with Oliver giving the young prince a bloody nose.

More certain is the surviving evidence concerning Cromwell's early education. As a boy, the clergyman and schoolmaster Dr Thomas Beard taught him at the local grammar school. Beard was author of the best-selling book *A Theatre of Judgement*, which offered a fierce warning to all sinners of the nature of God's wrath. Contrary to his moralizing tone, however, Beard was a notoriously self-serving man. He was a pluralist, grabbing as many offices, not to mention salaries, as he could get his hands on. Beard was not the kind of man who is likely to have fired Cromwell's later godly spirit, indeed Oliver would come to have very public disagreements with Beard over the latter's greedy desire for a local preaching lectureship in the late 1620s.[2]

With this solid educational grounding, Cromwell entered Sidney Sussex College at the University of Cambridge just two days before his seventeenth birthday. According to the scurrilous post-Restoration writings of James Heath, Cromwell was an unruly undergraduate: 'He was more Famous for his Exercises in the Fields than in the Schools, (in which he never had the honour of, because no worth and merit to, a degree) being one of the chief Match-makers and Players at Foot-ball, Cudgels, or any other boisterous sport or game'.[3] Heath portrays Cromwell living the ideal student lifestyle; practising 'uncontrolled debaucheries... Drinking, Wenching, and the like outrages of licentious youth'. Such lewd stories are a product of the same wave of resentment that caused the bodies of Cromwell, Ireton and Bradshaw to be exhumed in 1661. Heath's invented biography of Cromwell is on a par with the base ballads and bawdy tracts of the Restoration era. In reality, little is known of Cromwell's time at Sidney Sussex, apart from that it was short-lived. Following the death of his father, Oliver quit his studies at Cambridge in order to return home and take over the running of his family's property interests around Huntingdon; his next stay in the college would not be for another 340 years. With a widowed mother, not to mention seven unmarried sisters, to look after, the 18-year-old Oliver was taken from the quiet quadrangles of Cambridge and thrust into the hectic role of family management.

He also started a family of his own. On 22 August 1620 Cromwell married Elizabeth Bourchier, the daughter of a wealthy London fur trader and considerable landowner in Essex. The marriage brought Cromwell into the circle of some of the most 'godly' families in the country, placing him in a kinship network that included many important future Parliamentarian figures such as the Earl of Warwick and Oliver St John. Although very little evidence survives, Oliver and Elizabeth seemed to have had a happy marriage with nine children in total—five sons and four daughters. Life in Huntingdon, however, would not continue serenely for long. Within a decade of Cromwell's marriage, both he and his family were forced to leave Huntingdon for pastures new.

This change of fortunes was part of a wider decline in the local influence of the Cromwell clan. In 1627, Oliver's uncle was forced to sell Hinchingbrook House to pay off spiralling debts. The buyer was Sidney Montagu, brother to the Earl of Manchester. It was an important sea change in local politics that marked the rise of the Montagus and the fall of the Cromwells in Huntingdon. Although Oliver was elected MP for Huntingdonshire in 1628, getting his first taste of Parliament, there were already signs that Cromwell was beginning to feel the strain of his declining political and financial fortunes. While in London for the Parliamentary session, Oliver consulted Dr Theodore Mayerne, a London physician, who diagnosed him as suffering from a form of depression. On his return, things did not improve with a series of local disputes going against Cromwell. He argued vehemently against money from the bequest of a recently deceased townsman being siphoned off to pay for the lectureship of his erstwhile schoolmaster Beard. Instead, he demanded in vain that the money be used to fund a new lectureship for a fierier 'puritan' preacher. More seriously, the Montagus consolidated their grip on local affairs by obtaining a fresh town charter for Huntingdon. Under the new arrangement, the town's council was to be elected by an oligarchy of men sympathetic to the Montagus and excluding Cromwell. Incensed by what he saw as a blatant attempt by the new town rulers to promote their own selfish ends, Cromwell made vociferous complaints of malpractice against the Montagus. Cromwell's situation, however, did not improve and his outspoken accusations merely got him hauled before the privy council in December 1630.

Although Cromwell's decision to leave Huntingdon was not solely on the basis of these disputes, they did indicate further his sliding social status and inability to keep a political grip over local affairs. In May 1631 Cromwell sold his family's properties for the modest sum of £1,800. His sombre journey from his birthplace would not be a long one, however, as he and his family moved just five miles away, to the rural backwater of St Ives. No longer a landowning gentlemen, Cromwell now rented a small farm and lived as a yeoman farmer. His landlord was the godly gentleman Henry Lawrence—a man whom Cromwell would later repay by making him president of his Protectoral privy council. Cromwell's claim to have not quite lived in 'obscurity' was to be severely tested during this phase of his life.

It was around, or just before, the time of his move to St Ives that Cromwell underwent something of a religious conversion. Facing ruin in Huntingdon and fleeing into the flat, marshy, wilderness of the Cambridgeshire countryside, Cromwell found God. His experience is recounted in vivid detail in a letter of 1638 to his cousin Elizabeth St John:

> [God] giveth springs in a dry and barren wilderness where no water is... Truly no poor creature hath more cause to put forth himself in the cause of his God than I... The Lord accept me in His Son, and give me to walk in the light, and give us to walk in the light, as He is the light. He it is that enlighteneth our blackness, our darkness... He giveth me to see light in His light. One beam in a dark place hath exceeding much refreshment in it: blessed be His Name for shining upon so dark a heart as mine! You know what my manner of life hath been. Oh, I lived in and loved darkness,

and hated the light; I was a chief, the chief of sinners. This is true: I hated godliness, yet God had mercy on me. O the riches of His mercy.[4]

How extensive Cromwell's previous 'sins' were remains unknown, but they were unlikely to have been as egregious as the 'drinking, wenching, and the like outrages of licentious youth' outlined by Heath. The real sin for Cromwell was not seeing the light of God sooner. It was God that fortified Oliver and gave him guidance as he worked the land about St Ives. As he suffered through chronic bouts of bronchitis and malaria brought on by the damp fenland air, he put his faith in the Lord, just as he would on his deathbed in 1658. Here were the makings of that mindset that would propel him so prominently through the following two decades of political turmoil.[5]

By another twist of fate, and yet another family death, Oliver's fortunes improved in January 1636. The deceased was Cromwell's maternal uncle, Sir Thomas Steward. Dying childless, the majority of his landed interests around Ely, including the right to collect local tithes, passed to Oliver. He also inherited a large house on the edge of the cathedral green into which moved both Cromwell's family and his mother. Now on an annual income of nearly £300 a year, Cromwell had clawed his way back into the ranks of the lesser gentry.

Even in the late 1630s, Cromwell still displayed the traits of the moral crusader, which had seen him so roundly rebuked in Huntingdon. He supposedly opposed plans to drain and enclose large areas of fenland about the Isle of Ely because of the loss of livelihood it would bring for local inhabitants. One report suggests that those against the fen drainage scheme paid Cromwell 'a groat for every cow they had upon the common, to hold the drainers in suit for five years'. There is nothing to suggest that Cromwell was against enclosure in principle, much less a social revolutionary, but he was clearly keen to see that the commoners got a 'fair' deal out of it. The incident did give fuel to Cromwell's detractors, however. During the Civil War, the Royalists would come to label him 'Lord of the Fens'—a title that was intended to mock his low social upbringing.

During his years in obscurity Cromwell had, through marriage and kinship, formed powerful links with some of the most important puritan families in England. These were men who shared Cromwell's steadfast commitment to follow God's light; in particular, they believed that the Church of England was in need of a Reformation that went far beyond that of the sixteenth century. In 1640 Cromwell, now aged 41, would be elected to the so-called Long Parliament as member for the borough of Cambridge. In many ways, this election seems odd as it was usually reserved for a prominent resident of the town or a high standing Court official. Cromwell was neither of these. Indeed, despite his newfound wealth, he would have been one of the least affluent members in Parliament. Thus it seems likely that Cromwell's election was procured through the influence of his powerful allies.[6] Throughout that Parliament, Oliver can be seen operating on the peripheries of the faction that was driving forward opposition to the policies pursued by Charles I. Although Cromwell can in no way be said to have 'caused' the Civil War, he definitely made a small contribution to the melting pot of forces that would eventually put England into conflict.

The rise had been a remarkable one and would be even more incredible in the following two decades as he flourished into a Parliamentary commander and head of state. Arguably, however, it was these first 40 years of his life that were the making of the man. The sudden changes of fortune and bouts of illness hardened him for the uncertainties of later years. His experiences also brought about an intense religious experience that would fire his mental outlook for the rest of his life. Through marriage and friendship he had come to make powerful allies who would play a prominent part in his subsequent rise to fame. Overall, it can be said that Providence was certainly on Oliver's side.

In the same letter of 1638 in which Cromwell described his 'conversion' experience, Oliver also expressed one simple wish. Brooding under the shadow of Ely Cathedral he stated that: 'My soul is with the congregation of the firstborn, my body rests in hope, and if here I may honour my God either by doing or by suffering, I shall be most glad'.[7] Here was Cromwell in a waiting posture, unsure of where he would be going next. The late 1620s and 1630s had been times of 'suffering'; the Civil War was to mark the beginning of a time of 'doing'. Just like his head in death, Cromwell in life had fluctuating fortunes that at times were extremely perplexing. As he himself put it, 'No one rises so high as he who knows not whither he is going'.

* * *

Everybody 'knows' that Cromwell was a killjoy. He was the quintessential 'Roundhead'; plain in appearance, puritanical in nature, he wasn't exactly thrilling company. He would have had little in common with the drunken actor Samuel Russell, who owned his head in the late eighteenth century. Cromwell hated drink and he disliked fun. This 'popular' reputation, however, is apocryphal—mainly a caricature invented by bitter Royalists. He became something of a pantomime villain; responsible for all that was perceived 'wrong' with the Parliamentarian side. Over the years, this image has become so entrenched that myth and legend have almost become historical 'fact'. The country-wide perception of Cromwell as the destroyer of churches and cathedrals, for instance, has arisen through confusion of Oliver with Thomas Cromwell, the man who carried out Henry VIII's dissolution of the monasteries a century before. Likewise, Cromwell's character and personality is another example of the mythology that has enveloped him. Yet under closer scrutiny, much of the received wisdom about Oliver's puritanical nature begins to evaporate before our eyes.

That is not to say that some elements of the 'puritanical' Cromwell are not true. The celebration of Christmas was indeed outlawed in 1647 and upheld throughout Oliver's reign as Lord Protector. Moreover, from the summer of 1655 through to early 1657 the most infamous period of godly dictatorship gripped the Cromwellian Protectorate. Known as the rule of the Major Generals, this experiment saw the country divided into 12 districts each under the jurisdiction of a military officer. Largely a response to a failed Royalist uprising in March 1655, each of these Major Generals was responsible for collecting a 'decimation' tax on known Royalists in their district in order to fund a militia force to protect local security. As the privy council contemplated the instructions to be issued to these military governors, however, they decided to widen their mandate into the realm of godly reform. As well as enforcing the decimation tax and marshalling the militia, they were to ensure that 'no horse-races, cock-fighting, bear-baiting, stage-plays, or any such unlawful assemblies be suffered or permitted' and make sure that 'all alehouses, taverns and victualling houses towards the outskirts of the said cities … be suppressed'.[8] Although such measures were ostensibly to ensure that secret meetings of Royalist conspirators would not occur under the cover of race meetings or in the shady environment of the alehouse, all this has gone to confirm the popular notion that the Cromwellian regime was simply not 'fun'.

This perception is also backed up by Cromwell's own 'plain' image. Yet his desire to be painted 'warts and all' may have been more the result of self-styling than a lack of self-awareness. Arguably, his plain, dour look was as much a fashion statement as the garish garbs of foppish Cavaliers. In almost every contemporary portrait of the Lord Protector, he is dressed in his 'trade-mark' black clothes with white collar. It was a declaration of piety, plainness and thriftiness—never forgetting his lowly roots. During the Civil War, Cromwell once famously declared that 'I had rather have a plain russet-coated captain that knows what he fights for, and loves what he knows, than that which you call a gentleman and is nothing else.'[9] In those years in St Ives, he had not been too far removed from such 'russet-coated' men. Even when he appeared in Parliament in November 1640, the roughness of his dress was a source of comment. According to Sir Philip Warwick's *Memoirs*, Cromwell appeared 'Very ordinarily apparelled, for it was a plain cloth-suit, which seemed to have been made by an ill country tailor; his linen was plain, and not very clean, and I remember a speck or two of blood upon his little band, which was not much larger than his collar'.[10] In December 1653, for his inauguration as Lord Protector, he still displayed this lack of artifice and dressed simply in 'a black plush suit and cloak'.

Yet Oliver Cromwell was never quite as 'plain' as he

would have others believe. His mask of stern godliness often slipped during his reign as Lord Protector, thereby offering intriguing insights into Cromwell's character. The simple representations of Cromwell in portraiture, for example, did not tally with his lifestyle after 1653— maybe Robert Walker's colourful portrait of Oliver, now held in the Cromwell Museum, Huntingdon, captured another side to the man (see plate 19). From April 1654 until his death, Oliver and his family took up residence in the renovated rooms of the Palace of Whitehall.

As his reign went on, he would also take weekend breaks at Hampton Court. According to the diarist John Evelyn, Whitehall was 'very glorious and well furnished' under Cromwell.[11] Indeed, many of the late king's goods —including lavish tapestries and priceless paintings— were reinstalled at the orders of Cromwell and his council. Despite his perceived aversion to idolatry, Cromwell willingly consented to setting up a grand marble fountain in Hampton Court's privy garden—complete with statues of Venus, Cleopatra, Adonis and Apollo.[12] These were truly opulent surroundings, a world away from his modest upbringing in the Cambridgeshire fens. When it came to art and architecture, Cromwell's court was just as vibrant as any of its predecessors.

It was also an impressively large court.[13] The ranks of household servants that marched at Cromwell's funeral in November 1658 are testament enough to that. It may not have been quite on the same scale as monarchical predecessors, but it was by no means measly. The various departments typical in royal households, such as the wardrobe and the office of the works, remained. There were numerous artisans, including carpenters, masons, joiners, upholsterers, tailors, cobblers and hatters. There was also an impressive protectoral stables, presided over by Oliver's son-in-law John Claypole; a 'master of the barges' with a staff of 27 'watermen' garbed in coats bearing the Protectoral arms, entrusted with transporting the Protector and important visitors along the Thames; equally important were the Protector's guard of Halberdiers, which acted as Cromwell's personal bodyguard, dressed in coats of grey cloth just like the old royal guards. This was hardly plain living.

Moreover 'official' representations of Cromwell also grated against his self-professed simplicity. Protectoral coinage featured Oliver's image on the obverse, depicted in an imperial pose complete with a crown of laurels. On the reverse was the Protectoral arms conspicuously topped by an imperial crown and encircled by the Latin motto of the Protectorate regime: *Pax Quaeritur Bello* ('peace is sought through war'). Just as regal was Oliver Cromwell's 'Great Seal'—a large wax seal used to endorse important warrants, grants and patents that is now held in the National Archives. On the one side, Cromwell is depicted on horseback dressed in armour, just like his royal predecessors (see plate 22). On the other side are the Protectoral arms, surmounted by a six-barred helmet of monarchy with a crown atop. Indeed, there were no less than three crowns depicted on the great seal—a startling fact given that Cromwell never wore a crown himself. Equally revealing was Cromwell's signature from 1653, examples of which can be found in the National Archives (see plate 21). Instead of 'O. Cromwell' he came to sign himself 'Oliver P', meaning 'Oliver Protector', thus dropping his surname in the regal style.

Perhaps the greatest example of the extent to which Cromwell shed his drab image in favour of more kingly attire was his second inauguration as Lord Protector under the pseudo-monarchical constitutional arrangements of the *Humble Petition and Advice*. Arriving at Westminster by Protectoral barge just before two o'clock in the afternoon of 26 June 1657, Cromwell first went to Parliament to give his formal assent to the new constitutional settlement. Following this, a great procession comprising of court officials, the mayor and aldermen of London, foreign envoys and civic officials made its way reverently to Westminster Hall. This building, which had witnessed the sentencing of a king and would display Cromwell's head just four years later, was about to witness a ceremony on a par with a royal coronation. Leading the way before Cromwell was the Earl of Warwick, bearing the sword of state. The heralds, dressed in their Protectoral tabards, officiated over the pageantry. Cromwell made his way to the upper end of the Hall, below the 'great window', where a raised and canopied 'chair of state' was set, probably using the very same 'coronation chair' that had been utilized for the coronation of English sovereigns since the early fourteenth century.

One by one, the Speaker of the Commons bestowed upon Cromwell the symbols of office. First, according to the newspaper reports, was a 'robe of purple velvet, lined with ermine, being the habit anciently used at the solemn investiture of Princes'. Following this, Cromwell was presented with a richly gilt and embossed Bible, a sword and a solid gold sceptre—all that was missing was a crown. After taking his oath as Lord Protector, Oliver 'thus adorned in Princely State', must have wondered whether he really had turned down the offer of kingship just a month earlier. The gathered assembly gave 'several great shouts', and to the sound of trumpets Cromwell sat in the chair of state, 'holding the sceptre in his hand'. A herald then stood up and gave a signal for the trumpets to sound a further three times before he proceeded to 'publish and proclaim his Highness Lord Protector of the Commonwealth of England, Scotland, and Ireland, and the Dominions and Territories thereunto belonging'. Shouts of 'God Save the Lord Protector' echoed around the hall as the ceremony came to a close.[14]

One should be wary about reading too much into this 'kingly' image of Cromwell. In many ways, it was just as 'false' as the constructions of plain, godly Oliver. Primarily, it was used as a means to secure and legitimate the Protectoral regime. Cromwell did not appropriate the style of monarchy because he sought to be king: he did it because it was what people *expected* from their head of state. Even though Cromwell had refused the Crown because of his godly scruples, he still realized the importance of tradition and history to his fellow countrymen. In the wake of the turmoil of regicide and the uncertainties of the republican rule of the Rump Parliament, people welcomed a return to known ways. Given that, hitherto, the nation had only ever known monarchy, it made sense to keep the iconography of the new regime as traditional as possible. In order to command obedience it was important to use familiar forms. As Cromwell himself admitted, 'people do love what they know', and it was monarchy that Englishmen knew best. Moreover, international considerations also necessitated regal opulence. It was important to have both lavish palaces and impressive ceremonials in order to entertain foreign ambassadors and to keep up with the courts of Europe. England should not be seen as the poor relation. It is perhaps instructive that throughout the pompous display of 26 June 1657, standing either side of Cromwell's 'throne' were the French and Dutch ambassadors. Oliver's own self-effacing style would not cut it on the international scene, where image was everything. Even if Cromwell was not a king, it was important that he commanded the same respect as his predecessors.

Other seemingly frivolous facets of Cromwell's character, however, are less easily explained by political expediency. Despite godly chagrin against the 'beautification' of churches, not least the use of organ music in services, Cromwell seems to have enjoyed music away from places of worship. The Cromwellian Court included a 'master of music', seven other musicians and 'two lads brought up to music'.[15] Oliver even had the chapel organ removed from Magdalen College, Oxford, to the palace at Hampton Court for his own delectation. Even the hostile James Heath would concede that Cromwell was 'a great lover of music, and entertained the most skilful in his pay'.[16] Cromwell's attitudes to drink are also contradictory to supposed puritanical sobriety. The Venetian envoy Francesco Giavarina recounts one amusing story in May 1657. According to Giavarina, the Florentine resident had recently presented Oliver with 'a dozen butts of different wines, expressly sent from Tuscany'. The gift was wasted on Cromwell though, because: 'The Protector has no great taste for anything and he is not disposed to regard favourably presents of this character. One of his physicians has stated that he has not the courage to put such liquors to his lips.'[17] How much this distaste was down to Cromwell's dislike for alcohol is uncertain. As Giavarina admits, the wine had 'much deteriorated on the voyage' to England and may not have been in the most drinkable condition. On the other hand, Cromwell certainly drank beer. According to one commentator, Oliver 'drunk a cup of ale, and ate a piece of toast' before angrily dissolving his final parliament on 4 February 1658—perhaps it gave him a little courage in his difficult task.[18] Cromwell enjoyed music and liked the odd tipple; he was also not averse to parties as demonstrated by the festivities following the marriages of his daughters Frances and Mary.

Oliver's youngest daughter, Frances, married the grandson of the Earl of Warwick, Robert Rich on 11 November 1657. According to the Royalist, William Dugdale (no trustworthy source!) the celebrations that occurred the following day were sumptuous: 'On Thursday was the wedding feast kept at Whitehall where they had 48 violins and 50 trumpets and much mirth with frolics besides mixed dancing (a thing heretofore accounted profane) 'till 5 of the clock yesterday morning'. Equally lurid was another Royalist description of Cromwell's jovial and playful mood: 'The Protector threw about sack posset [a drink made from wine and milk] among all the ladies to soil their rich clothes, which they took as a favour ... and daubed all the stools where they were to sit with sweetmeats'. Oliver even chased the bridegroom and tugged off his periwig, 'and would have thrown it into the fire but he did not, yet he sat upon it'. An interesting anecdote, but it might be little more than that. Newsletter reports were guarded over the nature of the frivolities that accompanied the wedding, merely stating that 'the solemnities of the nuptials ... were kept with much privacy and honour, several of the nobility being then entertained according to their quality'.[19] Perhaps behind closed doors, and in such exalted company, Cromwell felt able to let his hair down.

Just one week later, at Hampton Court Palace, Mary Cromwell married Thomas Belasyse, Viscount Fauconberg. Cromwell's recently appointed Latin secretary and eminent poet, Andrew Marvell, wrote *Two Songs at the Marriage of the Lord Fauconberg and the Lady Mary Cromwell* especially for the occasion. It was a very weak revival of the great 'masques' that had graced the courts of the early Stuart kings. Probably set to music provided by the musicians of the Cromwellian court, the Lord Protector himself may have participated in the performance. Drinking, frolicking and even possibly acting, Cromwell definitely had more in common with Samuel Russell than might be first imagined.

Besides these jovial festivities, anecdotal evidence also suggests that Cromwell had a sense of humour, albeit a very idiosyncratic one. In times of tension, a burlesque, childish playfulness seems to have overridden Cromwell's stoic demeanour. In early 1648, for example, while Cromwell and other army officers were in a meeting discussing the future settlement of the nation, the Republican Edmund Ludlow claims that Oliver suddenly 'took up a cushion and flung it at my head, and then ran down the stairs'. Ludlow for his part grabbed another cushion and threw it at the fleeing Cromwell, almost causing him to 'hasten down faster than he desired'.[20] Splatters of ink rather than pillows were exchanged in January 1649 as the commissioners of the High Court of Justice came to sign the king's death warrant. According to Colonel

Ewer's later account Cromwell, taking the pen in his hand, 'marked Mr [Henry] Marten in the face with it, and Mr Marten did the like to him'. The lawyer, Bulstrode Whitelocke, remembered how in the company of a few trusted friends, huddled in a smoke-filled room, Cromwell was not averse to 'laying aside his greatness'. Being 'exceedingly familiar' with his company, he would 'by way of a diversion make verses with them, and every one must try his fancy'. As with the descriptions of the wild parties after Frances Cromwell's wedding, however, all these accounts, tainted by the lens of retrospection, might simply be hostile commentary.

Yet, even in his letters and speeches there are some streaks of wit and humour. When speaking to a parliamentary committee in April 1657, for example, he dryly ridiculed the fact that, in the past, clergymen had been approved to preach in Wales without any knowledge of the indigenous language. If they 'could understand Latin and Greek', Cromwell jibed, they were approved 'as if he spake Welsh'. In reality, so few of them understood Welsh that it 'went for Hebrew with a great many'.[21] At the other end of the scale, Cromwell could be quite insensitive when it came to cracking a joke. In August 1649, when writing to his son Richard's new wife, Dorothy, he added the following postscript: 'I hear thou didst lately miscarry. Prithee take head of a coach by all means; borrow thy father's nag when thou intendest to go abroad'.[22] Was Dorothy's miscarriage really the result of a riding accident? Without the full facts, the conclusion that this was a very bad pun from Oliver cannot be ignored. He also made merry with nicknames for his closest friends; dubbing, for example, the hardworking Hampshire gentleman, Richard Norton, as '*idle* Dick Norton'.[23] It was clearly a varied sense of humour, sometimes misunderstood and often lacking subtlety.

Taking all these strands of Cromwell's personality into account, it becomes obvious that he cannot be taken at face value. He preferred a plain style, but willingly took on himself a more 'kingly' image when required. He spent hours piously engaged in prayer, but also drank, joked and enjoyed music. It is these many contradictions in Cromwell's character that continue to make him so fascinating. He also wore many hats during his lifetime. He was a country farmer, a parliamentary General, a head of state and a committed father. It is to this final incarnation that the rest of the chapter shall be dedicated. Although Cromwell's life from the 1640s became increasingly public, he still prided himself on being a family man.

* * *

Family life was important for Cromwell. Even under the strain of the campaign or dealing with the laborious task of governing three nations, Cromwell did not lose touch with his family. He bargained hard for lucrative marriage alliances for his children. The marriage of his daughters Mary and Frances to Viscount Fauconberg and the heir of the Earl of Warwick, Robert Rich, in 1657 helped to place the Cromwells in a social network far removed from the farmstead in St Ives. That Cromwell loved his daughters is beyond doubt. His intense grief at the death of his second eldest daughter, Elizabeth Claypole, in August 1658 was arguably the factor that triggered his fatal illness.

Few letters survive between Cromwell and his wife, Elizabeth, but where we do catch a glimpse of their correspondence there is a loving tone. Writing while on campaign in Scotland in the early 1650s, Oliver assured Elizabeth, with words of tenderness that may sound a little strange today, that 'Thou art dearer to me than any creature'. Amid the butchery of the battlefield, Cromwell still had kinder thoughts for home. Indeed, Elizabeth's only criticism was that Cromwell spent too long away from his family. She only wished that Oliver would be able to come home, 'my life is but half a life in your absence', yet she willingly acquiesced in the fact that 'the providence of God' had grander plans for her husband.[24] When Cromwell took the reins of power from 1653 onwards, Elizabeth saw herself very much as a public figure. Often styling herself as 'her highness' or 'lady protectress', she accompanied her husband to many of the grand state ceremonies of the Protectorate.

Perhaps the best glimpse into Cromwell's family life, however, is provided by his relationship with his two surviving sons, Richard and Henry. Although the younger of the two, it was Henry Cromwell who was the more

PLATE 12: This lavishly illustrated account of public money received and paid in Ireland in the 1650s features a portrait of Cromwell. (TNA SP 63/281)

Know all Men by these Presents That I
Samuel Russell of Keppel Street in the Parish of Saint Saviour in
the County of Surry as well for and in Consideration of the
Sum of One Hundred & one Pounds heretofore advanced
to me by James Cox of Shoe Lane in the City of London Jeweller as for and
in Consideration of the farther Sum of Seventeen Pounds
making together the Sum of One Hundred eighteen Pounds to me in Hand
paid by the said James Cox at and before the Sealing and delivery of
these Presents / The Receipt of which said several Sums of Money I the said
Samuel Russell do hereby acknowledge and thereof and therefrom and of and
from the same respectively and every part thereof do acquit release and discharge
the said James Cox his Executors and Administrators for ever by these Presents)
Have Bargained and Sold released granted and confirmed and by these Presents
Do Bargain and Sell release grant and confirm unto the said James Cox All
that Scull or Head supposed to be the Scull or Head of Oliver Cromwell To
have and to hold the said Scull or Head unto and to the only Use and
Behoof of the said James Cox his Executors Administrators and Assigns
absolutely for ever freely and without any Interruption or Disturbance
whatsoever of from or by me the said Samuel Russell or any other Person or
Persons whomsoever And I the said Samuel Russell for myself my Executors
and Administrators do by these Presents Covenant and promise That I the said
Samuel Russell shall and will Warrant and for ever Defend the said Scull
or Head unto the said James Cox his Executors Administrators and Assigns against
me the said Samuel Russell my Executors and Administrators and against all and
every other Person and Persons whomsoever And I the said Samuel Russell have
put the said James Cox in full Possession of the said Scull or Head by delivering him
the same at the time of the Sealing and delivery hereof In Witness whereof I
the said Samuel Russell have hereunto set my Hand and Seal the Thirty eth
day of April in the Year of our Lord one thousand seven hundred and
eighty seven —

Sealed and Delivered and Livery and Seisin of the
said Scull or Head given to the said James Cox by   Sam.ˡ Russell
the said Samuel Russell, delivering the same to the
said James Cox in the Presence of

PLATE 13: The deed of assignment between James Cox and Samuel Russell,
dated April 1787. Russell sold Cromwell's head for 'one hundred and eighteen
pounds', later claiming that Cox tricked him out of his family heirloom.

PLATE 14, *right*: A drawing of Cromwell's head from the late eighteenth century. Interestingly, the head's appearance seems to have changed little through the eighteenth century (see also plate 15) to its eventual burial in 1960.

PLATE 15, *below*: The cover of John Cranch's pamphlet for the 1799 exhibition of Cromwell's head, complete with the author's own drawing of the head. Entry cost two shillings and sixpence, but the show proved to be a complete failure.

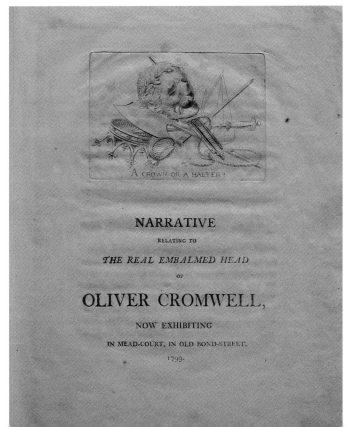

A CROWN OR A HALTER?

NARRATIVE

RELATING TO

THE REAL EMBALMED HEAD

OF

OLIVER CROMWELL,

NOW EXHIBITING

IN MEAD-COURT, IN OLD BOND-STREET.

1799.

PLATE 16, *left*: Comparisons of Cromwell's head with his life mask (*below*). After taking into account the head's shrinkage after 300 years of decay, 'cranial detectives' Pearson and Morant found an almost exact match — warts and all!

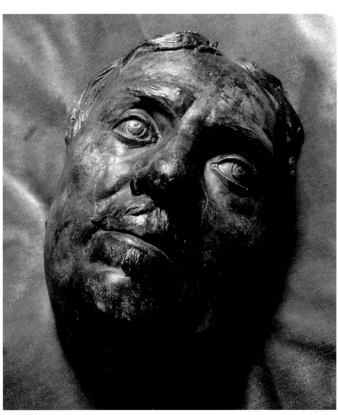

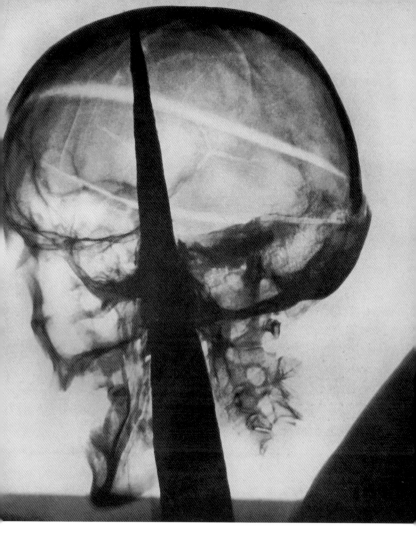

PLATE 17, *left*: The life mask of Oliver Cromwell, made from a plaster cast of Oliver's face during his lifetime. Thought to date from the mid-1650s, this was one of several busts, masks and portraits used by Pearson and Morant to unravel the mystery of Cromwell's head.

PLATE 18, *above*: An X-ray of Cromwell's head taken in 1934. The tip of the metal prong on which the head was displayed above Westminster Hall is clearly lodged in the skull.

PLATE 19, *right*:
This portrait of Oliver Cromwell by Robert Walker, *c.*1650, shows him dressed in a surprisingly elaborate style — complete with plumed hat and petticoat breeches. Such lavish clothing contradicted his self-professed austerity.

PLATE 20, *below*:
Letters Patent of Richard Cromwell dated October 1658, including a portrait of the new Lord Protector. Although appropriating his image, Richard failed to live up to his father as Lord Protector. He would later be ridiculed as 'Tumble Down Dick'.
(TNA E407/182)

PLATE 21, *right*:
Cromwell's signature
on a commission to
Major General William
Boteler, October 1655.
While Lord Protector,
Oliver signed himself
'Oliver P', very much
in the style of a mon-
arch. (TNA SP 27/2)

PLATE 22, *right*:
Oliver Cromwell's
Great Seal, held by
the National Archives,
depicts the Lord
Protector in regal
style in armour on
horseback. Oliver
seems to have realized
the importance
of appropriating
'traditional' styles as a
means of commanding
enduring authority.

PLATE 23, *right*: The plaque marking the burial of Cromwell's head at Sidney Sussex College, Cambridge. The interment on 25 March 1960 was a private affair, attended by only seven people, and the head's exact location remains a secret.

Near to this place was buried on 25 March 1960 the head of OLIVER CROMWELL Lord Protector of the Commonwealth of England, Scotland & Ireland, Fellow Commoner of this College 1616-7

PLATE 24 : Canon Horace Wilkinson in *c.*1949 holding his prized possession. The Wilkinson family were guardians of Cromwell's head from 1815 to 1960; after Canon Wilkinson's death his son donated it to Sidney Sussex College.

prominent figure in Cromwell's own lifetime. It was from Henry's marriage to Elizabeth, eldest daughter of Oliver's close friend Sir Francis Russell, in 1653 that the impecunious actor Samuel Russell would claim descent. Unlike his elder brother, Henry saw service on the battlefields of the Civil War and spent most of the 1650s in an important political role as effective governor of Ireland. He was definitely a chip off the block, not just in military service but also in his spiritual outlook. In 1651, while in Ireland, one correspondent informed Oliver of how Henry was undergoing a 'conversion' experience not unlike that of his father: 'I have had great encouragement that the word of God takes great effect upon him; he hath had inward temptations in his soul, and many words of grace made very precious and comfortable to his soul, and I watch him, and he is much crying to God in secret'.[25] Both godly and militarily experienced, he was the perfect son for Oliver Cromwell. Despite all this, however, Oliver never really made an effort to promote his son in England. From July 1655, Henry languished in the thankless task of Irish administration, never to return home before his father's death in September 1658. It was 'an honourable banishment' as Henry would later reflect bitterly.[26] Moreover, Oliver was very cagey about bestowing much-needed titles and authority on Henry. It seems he was always nervous of accusations of 'favouritism' among his friends and relations. Oliver refused, for instance, to strip his son-in-law, Charles Fleetwood, of the title of Lord

Deputy of Ireland in favour of Henry, despite Fleetwood being permanently recalled to England from 1655. Not until November 1657, when Fleetwood's commission finally expired, would Oliver grant the office to his son.

Compared to Henry, Richard Cromwell must have been a disappointment to his father. From February 1648 through to April 1649, Cromwell haggled with Richard Maijor, a member of the Hampshire gentry, for his son's marriage to Maijor's eldest daughter, Dorothy. Although the Maijor's were actually a pretty minor family, Oliver refused more lucrative offers of marriage for his eldest son because they did not come 'with the assurance of godliness' that this match would bring.[27] According to Oliver, reports of Dorothy's 'godliness and virtue' had 'so great a place in my heart'.[28] Richard needed straightening out, and the Maijor's were just the family to do it. Dorothy and Richard married at Maijor's estate at Hursley in Hampshire on 1 May 1649, just before Oliver left for his infamous campaign in Ireland.

Richard fitted well into the life of a Hampshire country gentleman. He was named a Justice of the Peace and dealt with various local administrative affairs. For Oliver, however, Richard was growing too comfortable in his 'idle' lifestyle. As he boarded ship at Milford Haven in August 1649, ready to set sail for Ireland, his thoughts were still on Richard. Writing to Richard Maijor, Cromwell urged him to keep an eye on his son: 'I have committed my son to you; pray give him advice… I would have him mind and understand business, read a little history, study the mathematics and cosmography: these are good, with subordination to the things of God. Better than idleness, or mere outward worldly contents'.[29] Richard's expensive, carefree living grated against Oliver's godly nature. Cromwell even appealed to his new daughter-in-law to take care of her husband's spiritual wellbeing:

> I desire you both to make it above all things your business to seek the Lord: to be frequently calling upon Him, that He would manifest Himself to you… He will be speaking in your ear and in your heart, if you attend thereunto. I desire you to provoke your husband likewise thereunto. As for the pleasures of this life, and outward business, let that be upon the bye.[30]

Although Oliver's concerns for Richard have all the hallmarks of an overbearing father, they also betray his heartfelt need to watch over the spiritual care of his family.

Following Oliver's rise to head of state, he tried to encourage his eldest son to take a more active role in public life. Richard was elected Member of Parliament, for instance, in both 1654 and 1656. In December 1657, by his father's nomination, Richard was made a lord of the Protectoral 'Other House' or upper chamber of Parliament. Yet despite his presence at Westminster, he made little impact. He merely took a back seat, listening to, and being guided by, others. Likewise, Oliver promoted Richard to his privy council in December 1657, thus allowing him a position in the inner sanctum of government policy making. Some contemporaries were led to believe that all these promotions were signs that Cromwell had Richard lined up for the top job. One vitriolic pamphlet from early 1658, for example, sensed that Richard was considered 'very likely to be his father's successor'.[31]

They clearly did not understand Oliver. Under the Parliamentary constitution of 1657 by which Cromwell was invested as Protector, he was expected to 'appoint and declare the person who shall immediately after your death succeed you in the Government of these nations'. Just because Cromwell gave his eldest son a bit more responsibility, however, should not be taken as firm evidence that he designed him as his political successor. He would have been mad to consider bestowing the running of government to one so inexperienced. Moreover, Richard's spiritual failings and questionable character would have remained troubling to his father. As one critical account jeered, Richard was 'well skilled in Hawking, Hunting, Horse-racing, with other sports and pastimes', but he was not skilled in politics or the ways of God. Maybe Cromwell was trying to keep Richard busy and, more importantly, under his direct supervision, by giving him a number of key positions in the centre of government. More experienced men such as Oliver's son-in-law Charles Fleetwood, or Richard's younger brother Henry, were much more suitable candidates for the next Lord Protector.

Throughout his career, Cromwell had been vehemently against hereditary succession. He did not relish the accusations of self-seeking and hypocrisy that would accompany setting up the Lord Protectorship in his own family. In a stormy speech at the dissolution of the First Protectorate Parliament on 22 January 1655, Oliver gave a clear warning to those who wanted to set the Protectorate on a hereditary footing. According to Cromwell, if the office of Lord Protector had been placed 'in my family hereditarily, I would have rejected it'. Quoting scriptural authority, Cromwell stressed that it was fit 'to have men chosen, for their love to God, and to Truth and Justice; and not to have it hereditary. For as it is in *Ecclesiastes*: "Who knoweth whether he may beget a fool or wise"?'[32] Cromwell's aversion to the hereditary principle explains its omission from the *Humble Petition and Advice*. He liked the new constitution because it did not set up 'Hereditary Lords, nor Hereditary Kings'.[33] To choose Richard as his successor would have forced Cromwell to go against his own godly principles.

It is difficult to escape the conclusion that Oliver never actually chose Richard as his successor. The stories of Cromwell's deathbed nomination all derive from the period following his death on the fateful afternoon of 3 September. Indeed, before he died there appears to have been a number of frantic but unsuccessful attempts, not least by Secretary of State John Thurloe, to get Cromwell to formally designate his successor. Cromwell was implored to put his choice in a formal document under his seal but, through a potent mixture of feverish fits, political considerations and an unwillingness to tempt God, he refused. Late on the evening of Monday 30 August, Thurloe wrote to Henry Cromwell to vent his anxieties. He feared the repercussions for the Protectoral regime 'if his highnesse should not settle and fix his successor before he dyes', adding crucially, 'which truely I beleeve he hath not yet done'. If Cromwell did not 'settle his succession before his death, the judgment would be the soarer, and our condition the most dangerous'. The situation was 'an absolute secret' and he beseeched Henry to 'keepe it so'.[34] With uncertainty and fear rife at Whitehall, the final few days of Cromwell's life were spent in an admixture of prayer and desperate discussion. As Oliver's condition declined, however, so did any hope of that crucial nomination being made.

Only when Cromwell had died did stories start to emerge about Richard's 'nomination'. Yet the accounts coming from Whitehall were confusing, contradictory and, most importantly, lacked any tangible evidence to support them. Only reference to a feeble 'verbal' designation—encompassing anything from a cursory nod to a fully coherent statement from the dying Protector—was given as evidence of Richard's right to succeed his father. Most astonishing was the narrative provided by Thurloe the day after Cromwell's death. Once again he wrote to Henry, but could now categorically state that 'His highness was pleased before his death to declare my lord Richard successor', perplexingly adding that 'He did it upon munday'.[35] This was the same Monday on which Thurloe had written late to Henry to tell him that he believed no nomination had or would be made! Likewise, Thurloe had written to Henry on Tuesday 31 August, restating his despair over Oliver's condition and his inability of doing anything 'respectinge to the publique'.[36] If, as Thurloe was now claiming on 4 September, Oliver had declared Richard his successor 'upon munday', why had he not revealed this fact on Monday night or Tuesday? His despair before Cromwell's death betrays the lies he constructed after it.

It seems as though with Oliver dead and no successor named, those around his deathbed took it on themselves to choose a successor. A three-hour meeting of the privy council ensued in which the 'evidence' for Richard's nomination was weighed up. Eventually it was resolved unanimously or 'nemine contradicente' that '*it appears* to the Counsel, that his late Highness hath appoynted, and Declared the Lord Richard Cromwell, his eldest Sonn, to be Lord Protector'. The lack of conviction is highly suggestive of the fact that no nomination had really been made. To give the feeble resolution a little more weight, the order book states 'that the former Vote be entered', and in particular reiterates that there be 'notice taken therein, that the same passed, nemine contradicente'.[37] The following day Richard Cromwell was proclaimed as

Lord Protector across the capital. The trumpets sounded at Whitehall as the heralds performed their traditional duties just as they had at Oliver's inauguration a year earlier, including the reading aloud of the proclamation and leading the shouts of 'God save His Highness Richard Lord Protector' (see plate 20).

Yet why did the council agree to this charade? It seems that those at the centre of the Cromwellian regime believed Oliver's son was the safest option for all concerned. For the conservative elements on the council, Richard was an affable country squire who shared their grievances against unbridled military rule. For the army grandees, Richard was a pliable relative—brother-in-law to Lieutenant-General Charles Fleetwood and nephew of General John Desborough—and could therefore be worked from behind in the army's interests. By placing the succession in the eldest son of the Lord Protector, they also ensured that there would be little dispute over the novel notion of 'elective' succession to the supreme magistracy. They had effectively substituted elective succession with a hereditary one. It was seen as the best way to ensure the survival of the Protectoral regime.

The plan failed. Richard failed to live up to the expectations of the military grandees. Just two weeks into his reign as Lord Protector, Fleetwood, accompanied by a group of army officers, presented an address to Richard, with the ominous wish that he would 'inherit not only your Father's glory and authority, but also the hearts of his old faithful followers'. They likewise hoped that the 'blessing of the God of your Father' would continue with Richard.[38] Already the weaknesses of Richard's character were starting to worry the army. Even though Oliver had granted the command of a cavalry regiment to Richard in January 1658, he was no soldier. He had not fought on the battlefields of the Civil War and did not understand army politics. The same lack of religious fervour that had vexed his father over a decade before was still troubling the army officers. Instead, Richard leaned heavily on conservative 'civilian' advisors who looked disdainfully on military interference in the government. He was incapable of striking the same sort of balance between the military and civilian factions that had been the lynchpin of Oliver's success. By turning his back on the military, Richard effectively brought about his own downfall.[39]

Surely Oliver Cromwell would have apprehended that this would be the outcome of nominating his son as his successor. From early on he had realized that Richard was a 'problem child', lacking the godly convictions that had driven himself to take up arms in the 1640s and sustained him through the turmoil of the 1650s. In reality, the story of Cromwell's nomination of Richard should be regarded as much as a slur on his character as the vile representations of the Restoration regime. In death, his head might pass through generations of the Russell and Wilkinson families by hereditary descent; in life, however, he was adamant that the Protectorate would not be 'Cromwellian' beyond his lifetime. Oliver loved his family but he did not aim to set it up as the ruling dynasty.

*   *   *

Cromwell was clearly a complex character even in his own lifetime. Both extremes of Cromwell's image—on the one hand the dour puritan, on the other the 'king in all but name'—were equally fictitious. They were public relations exercises of which the publicist John Cranch would have been proud. Yet the 'real' Cromwell probably rested somewhere between these poles. Without doubt he was sincerely 'godly' in nature, but that did not mean he could not enjoy life. He might have risen from relative obscurity but he did not spend his life living in penitential squalor. Moreover, the 'public' man did not always run congruous to the 'private'. His mask of stern authoritarianism while Lord Protector, or his ruthlessness on the battlefield as Parliamentary commander, went against his tenderness and loving nature as a father. Cromwell was never one-dimensional. Just as people gazed upon his head in death and took a sceptical stance over its authenticity, the same should be true of Cromwell in life. Like the head, it was not enough to judge him by a glance at his outward features.

Following his death, however, Oliver Cromwell has become even more contested. Each generation has taken certain facets of his character, actions and image to create its own representation of Cromwell. The result has been

This was an age in which the scurrilous account of Cromwell's life given in James Heath's *Flagellum* could truly flourish.[1]

As the years passed by, and the elements eroded the distinctive features of his head, attitudes towards Cromwell also softened a little. His head may still have commanded a prominent view on the London skyline, but the significance of the man behind it faded. Civil War passed out of living memory, as did the acts of Cromwell and his regime. The head's removal from Westminster Hall around the 1680s perfectly parallels attitudes to Cromwell's memory as a whole. He disappeared into a momentary anonymity, remembered only in the popular imagination as a shadow of the hostile post-Restoration caricature. Cromwell became a bogeyman invoked to frighten young children. From the late seventeenth century, he was even the subject of a popular nursery rhyme that began with the lines:

> Oliver Cromwell lay buried and dead,
>> Hee-haw, buried and dead,
> There grew an old apple tree over his head,
>> Hee-haw, over his head.[2]

In reality, his head was not buried, nor was his memory quite dead. For the moment, the head sat prominently among the curiosities of Du Puy's private museum; but its meaning had partially become detached from feelings about the man in life. It was an interesting object in itself, a grisly curio of a bygone age, rather than a sacred relic of a great man.

Cromwell would not be kept down for long though. By the 1690s, interest in the late Lord Protector was reignited by the publication of a number of 'memoirs' written by key figures of the 1640s and 1650s. These included men such as the self-serving lawyer, Bulstrode Whitelocke; the bitter Republican, Edmund Ludlow; and the frustrated godly minister, Richard Baxter. All of them talked of their ambivalent relationships with Oliver. They trace the mounting temptations that worked on Cromwell's soul, driving him to gain power no matter what the costs to his former friends and the cause for which they had fought. It formed a persuasive and pervasive narrative of a good man turned bad. These voices, however, were by no means authentic. Ludlow's *Memoirs*, in particular, were heavily edited in places to deliberately highlight the gulf between the honest Republican and the scheming Machiavellian. The impact of these memoirs would both propagate and entrench the unfavourable opinion towards Oliver Cromwell for the following century.

Yet, despite the vituperative tone of these works, they never equalled the shameless slurs of the Restoration period. Even in the most damning accounts there were cursory concessions to Cromwell's achievements. Most notable was Clarendon's *History of the Rebellion*, first published in 1702. Edward Hyde, earl of Clarendon had been a Royalist during the Civil Wars and had lived in exile with Charles II during the Cromwellian Protectorate. At face value, he would hardly seem the most likely person to take a favourable view on Oliver. Indeed, he charged Cromwell with 'all the wickedness against which damnation is denounced and hell-fire is prepared'. Somewhat surprisingly, however, Clarendon then goes on to admit that his former adversary, for all his faults, possessed 'a great spirit, an admirable circumspection and sagacity, and a most magnanimous resolution'. In foreign affairs, Cromwell outstripped the Stuart kings: 'His greatness at home was but a shadow of the glory he had abroad. It was hard to discover which feared him most, France, Spain or the Low Countries'. Perhaps most memorable was Clarendon's ultimate conclusion of Cromwell as 'a brave bad man'. This one phrase sums up the prevailing attitude towards Cromwell for the rest of the eighteenth century. The acts Cromwell had committed were undoubtedly wrong, but the dynamism with which he had carried them out was almost admirable.

Even as the eighteenth century drew to a close, there were very few who viewed Cromwell in a completely favourable light. By now, Cromwell's head was on display once more. Passing from Samuel Russell to James Cox and then on to the Hughes brothers—the moment had come for the great show on Bond Street. It was perhaps no coincidence that the year this spectacle occurred was 1799—the 200th anniversary of Cromwell's birth. John Cranch's brief narrative on the head's history was unashamedly praising towards its erstwhile owner: 'In his time the most intrepid and victorious general, the most sagacious statesman and the most powerful sovereign, in Europe … who at last, yielding only to death, left behind him a name which cannot be extinguished but in that oblivion which shall bury the memory of all human actions'.[3] It was a laudatory tone ahead of its time. That the show would flop is probably indicative of the fact that not everybody shared Cranch's favourable opinion—not to mention the expensive entry fee! The hostile mood continued into the early nineteenth century. Following the French Revolution and Bonaparte's *coup d'état*, the inevitable, unflattering comparisons with Cromwell and his regime were rife. Both were cast in the roles of opportunistic schemers, striving to satisfy their unbridled ambition. Around this time, Cromwell's head would be refused by the Piccadilly Museum, only to be snapped up by an obscure Kentish gentleman. Oliver's reputation still lay in the doldrums.

By 1899, the tercentenary of Oliver's birth, all this had changed. Thousands gathered in London to mark the event. Numerous statues and paintings were unveiled depicting the great Lord Protector. Many biographies were published around that time with a praising tone a world away from the invective of the Restoration era. The transformation of Oliver Cromwell from villain to hero was complete. Still in the possession of the Wilkinson family, Cromwell's head had a new lease of life during this period.

The media, riding this wave of 'Cromwellianism', started to take a keen interest in the unusual item—much to the mortification of Wilkinson. People began talking of a permanent shrine to Oliver, with the head either interred or prominently displayed to complete the monument. In this climate, pressure mounted for a 'forensic' investigation of the head's authenticity. Once the head was proven 'real', it could then take its place in some public commemorative work.

Yet, if 1899 marked the apex of the Cromwellian vogue, it was 1845 that saw the beginning of this trend. The trailblazer was the historian Thomas Carlyle: the man who had written off William Wilkinson's head in 1849 as 'fraudulent moonshine'. Four years earlier, the publication of his *Letters and Speeches of Oliver Cromwell* was a major contributor to the rehabilitation of Cromwell's reputation. Its genius came from the fact that it let Cromwell speak for himself—it laid bare Oliver's own words, allowing a glimpse into his thoughts and beliefs. Although Carlyle's own idiosyncratic interpolations among the text can sometimes distract, it is arguable that no historian since has come so close to capturing the 'true' Cromwell. Even to this day, scholars generally regard Carlyle's work as the best, and most accessible, printed source of Cromwell's words. It was a hit from the very beginning, selling-out almost immediately. Successive new editions were produced in order to meet demand. The impact was immense. Read by both high and low, and passed down the generations, thousands were given the opportunity to 'read' Cromwell for themselves. Carlyle defended Oliver's sincerity and his belief in God's guiding hand. The prevailing theme seems to be that Cromwell might have been flawed in many ways but he had integrity. Of course, Carlyle was not the first to expound these ideas, but he was the first to put them into such a comprehensive, widely read work.

That Carlyle's Cromwell came to have such an impact on Victorian England is largely the product of the society that embraced it. There was a ready willingness to accept this new, favourable interpretation of Cromwell's character because it appealed to a number of themes and interests emerging in Victorian England as a whole. Post-Restoration abuse aside, the revival of Cromwell in the Victorian age probably provides the clearest example of the reconstruction of a reputation based on the preoccupations of the time.

*　*　*

Cromwell's godly character struck a chord with Victorian sensibilities. By the second half of the nineteenth century this inherent 'puritanism' had become a prominent part of Cromwell's appeal. The fiercely virtuous, moral, upright Cromwell was something that most Victorian families could admire. His private devotion became an exemplar for all to follow. Most importantly, Oliver came to be identified as a forerunner in 'enlightened' thinking about religious toleration. It was generally believed that under his protection, Cromwell had allowed a freedom to worship unmatched until two centuries after his death.

Indeed, it was the Nonconformists who made the greatest claims over Cromwell's reputation. Baptist congregations, in particular, were quick to remember those halcyon days under Oliver Cromwell, compared to their subsequent repression and persecution during the post-Restoration era. Nonconformist historians began to write favourable accounts that stressed Cromwell's sincerity and faith. John Forster, for instance, fortified by the work of his close friend Carlyle, exalted Cromwell as 'No victim of ambition, no seeker after sovereignty or sovereign power... he was a man whose every thought was with the Eternal—a man of a great, robust, massive, mind and an honest, stout English heart'. By the 1870s Cromwell could be triumphantly described as 'the hero-saint of all true Baptists and Congregationalists'. Remarkably, given his antipathy to iconography in churches, Oliver even found himself depicted in the stained glass windows of Congregationalist chapels.[4]

This was a highly distorted image of Cromwell. To see him as some sort of champion of religious toleration is immensely anachronistic. Preoccupied with their own concerns for toleration in the late nineteenth century, Congregationalists traced their origins back to the mid-seventeenth century. Yet again, Oliver's reputation had been hijacked to meet the needs of the society that resurrected him. As we shall see, Cromwell's own attitudes to religious liberty were much less inclusive than his nineteenth-century admirers would like to admit. In order to view his attitudes to 'toleration' more clearly, it is necessary to follow Thomas Carlyle's lead and let Cromwell speak for himself.

On 4 July 1653, Cromwell delivered a three-hour speech to the so-called 'Barebones Parliament'. Following the forced expulsion of the Rump Parliament, this body of handpicked men was entrusted with finding a viable future settlement. Cromwell was arguably in his most fiery, 'millenarian', mood at this point of his life; his religious fervour comes across in this speech more than any other. A little over halfway through the oration, following a staunch defence of his actions against Parliament and praising the Providences of God, Oliver turned to the importance of finding settlement in religion:

> I beseech you … have a care for the whole flock! Love the sheep, love the lambs; love all, cherish and countenance all, in all things that are good. And if the poorest Christian, the most mistaken Christian, shall desire to live peaceably and quietly under you … if any shall desire but to lead a life in godliness and honesty, let him be protected.[5]

This was perhaps Oliver's most impassioned plea for religious 'toleration'. In reality, however, the 'flock' to which Cromwell wanted to extend this liberty was not exactly a broad one.

On 12 September 1654, Oliver found himself defending religious liberties to another Parliamentary assembly. This time, he did so as head of state — the Lord Protector of England, Scotland and Ireland under the army's *Instrument of Government*. Taking issue with the Parliament's unwillingness to accept the new constitutional arrangements, Cromwell gave a staunch defence of the 'fundamental' aspects of the *Instrument*. Among these non-negotiable points was 'liberty of conscience in religion', which was very much a 'natural right'.[6] What Cromwell meant by 'liberty of conscience' can be partially gleaned from Article 37 of the *Instrument*. It stated that:

> Such as profess faith in God by Jesus Christ … shall not be restrained from, but shall be protected in, the profession of the faith and exercise of their religion; so as they abuse not this liberty to the civil injury of others and to the actual disturbance of the public peace on their parts: provided this liberty be not extended to Popery or Prelacy, nor to such as, under the profession of Christ, hold forth and practise licentiousness.

It seemed to offer a lot, but in reality conceded very little. Clearly there were many that would be excluded from his vision of religious liberty, not least the Catholics. Instead, what Cromwell offered was a limited toleration aimed primarily at different strands of Protestantism. As he emphatically told Parliament in September 1656, 'If men will profess — be they those under Baptism, be they those of the Independent judgement simply, and of the Presbyterian judgement—in the name of God, encourage them … to make use of the liberty given them to enjoy their own consciences'.[7]

Moreover, Cromwell became increasingly annoyed by the bickering nature of the various religious sects. Liberty of conscience only worked if there was a *reciprocal* toleration between the sects. Yet, as Cromwell bitterly reflected, this was not the case:

> What is that which possesseth every sect? What is it? That every sect may be uppermost! That every sort of men may get the power into their hands… It is not that only; but we have an appetite to variety; to be not only making wounds, but widening those already made, as if we should see one making wounds in a man's side, and would desire nothing more than to be groping and grovelling with his fingers in those wounds![8]

Although Baptists might come to reflect on the mid-seventeenth century as the 'glory days' of toleration, the fact remains that there was much intolerance between the sects. Moreover, following Cromwell's acceptance of the *Humble Petition and Advice* in 1657, the religious freedom granted under the Protectorate became much tighter. The definition of the 'public profession' of faith was more restrictive. Oliver seemed to be shifting more markedly towards the religious conservatism of his civilian 'Presbyterian' allies.[9] The idealism of his speech of July 1653 had long gone.

Probably the most celebrated steps towards 'toleration' made by Cromwell were his attempts to secure the 're-admission' of the Jews into England in late 1655. King Edward I had officially expelled the Jews from England in 1290. Over 360 years later, Cromwell made steps to reverse this policy. The petition of an Amsterdam Jew named Menasseh ben Israel had first aroused his interest. On Cromwell's insistence, the document was brought before the privy council for discussion. He vigorously countered calls to reject the petition outright and assiduously attended every session of the council's subcommittee on the matter of re-admission in December 1655. As the opening gambit to this meeting, the Protectoral judges were asked to state the law concerning Jews. To the surprise of most sitting there they ruled that there was actually no law to prevent Jews from living in England. Unperturbed, merchants attending this conference vigorously argued against admitting Jews due to the commercial competition they would provide. According to one report, Cromwell merely retorted ironically: 'Can you really be afraid that this mean despised people should be able to prevail in trade and credit over the merchants of England, the noblest and most esteemed merchants of the world!'[10] Clergymen who attended the meeting raised fears that the construction of a synagogue in the capital might tempt Englishmen to convert to Judaism.

In the end the council sided with the opposition and refused to let Cromwell have his way. Behind the scenes, however, Cromwell acquired tacit toleration for the Jews. By 1656, a small group of Portuguese Jewish merchants resided in London with permission to worship in private houses and even acquire their own cemetery.

Yet Cromwell's concessions to the Jews were not exactly out of toleration for their religion. It stemmed from his belief, gleaned from his reading of the Bible, that the conversion of the Jews was a necessary prerequisite for the second coming of Christ. Cromwell had stressed to the council's subcommittee that he had no sympathy with the Jews but only sought to fulfil scriptural prophecy: 'Since there was a promise of their conversion, means must be used to that end, which was the preaching of the Gospel, and that could not be done unless they were permitted to dwell where the Gospel was preached'.[11] Admitting the Jews into England, where godliness abounded, would be the best way to convert them. By doing so, Cromwell hoped to be hastening the nation into a New Jerusalem. What Cromwell offered, therefore, was by no means toleration of Judaism.

More indicative of the limits of Cromwell's 'toleration' was the notorious case of the Quaker, James Nayler. On 24 October 1656, Nayler, in parody of Christ's entry into Jerusalem, had ridden into Bristol with a group of admiring female followers strewing his path with palms. Perhaps comical today, his crime in 1656 was extremely serious.

Following investigation by Bristol magistrates, his case was forwarded all the way up to Parliament. Nayler was a leading light in the emerging Quaker movement, believed to have 60,000 adherents by the end of the 1650s. To many, their beliefs seemed dangerous. They followed what their consciences told them was right—their 'inner light' as they called it—as this was held to be the voice of God. They stressed the importance of this 'inner light' over scripture—preferring to be guided by conscience rather than the Bible. Perhaps it was this belief that drove Nayler to his infamous deed. Fortified by the notion that God's light resides in all, Nayler saw nothing wrong in acting out the deeds of Christ.

When the matter came to be examined in Parliament in December 1656, however, few sympathized with Nayler. Paranoid about the growth of Quakerism, there were fears that Nayler's stunt was just the tip of an iceberg of subversion. Quakers came under suspicion not just for their unorthodox religious beliefs but also for their lack of deference to the traditional social order: they refused to remove their hats in the presence of superiors and even allowed women to preach before their congregations. Following the reading of a Parliamentary committee report on Nayler's activities, Major-General Philip Skippon rose to condemn the Quaker movement as a whole: 'It has been always my opinion, that the growth of these things is more dangerous than the most intestine or foreign enemies... Their great growth and increase is too notorious, both in England and Ireland; their principles strike both at ministry and magistracy'.[12] For Skippon, Nayler's crime was 'a horrid blasphemy' and should be punished as such. Major-General Boteler immediately seconded Skippon with an impassioned speech that left no doubt over what Nayler's fate should be: 'by the Mosaic law, blasphemers were to be stoned to death. The morality of this remains, and for my part, if this sentence should pass upon him, I could freely consent'.[13] This was hardly a shining example of Cromwellian toleration.

The attacks on Nayler inevitably descended into an examination of the toleration allowed by the Protectoral regime as a whole. Skippon saw the lax terms of the *Instrument of Government* as the route of the abounding sectarian excesses. He complained how 'these Quakers, Ranters, Levellers, Socinians, and all sorts, bolster themselves under [articles] thirty-seven and thirty-eight' of the *Instrument*.[14] Indeed, because the religious clauses of the *Instrument* were not strict enough, they could not be used to adequately punish Nayler's blasphemy. Alternative solutions were mooted; some declaring that Parliament should proceed by an act of attainder to condemn Nayler to death, others arguing that the House of Commons should use the judicial powers of the defunct House of Lords to try him. There was also a minority that counselled caution. Colonel Holland, for instance, urged the assembly to remember 'how many Christians were formerly martyred under this notion of blasphemy'.[15]

They had to be careful how they defined 'blasphemy' for otherwise other, more orthodox sects might fall under censure. This combination of legal and religious doubts meant that by a vote of 96 to 82 Nayler was spared execution. Instead he was to be branded, pilloried, whipped through the streets of London, have his tongue bored through and be imprisoned for life. A punishment that, the Speaker of the House assured Nayler, was for his 'reformation rather than destruction'.[16]

It should be noted that while this act of religious bigotry was brewing at Westminster, Oliver Cromwell remained conspicuously silent. Indeed, his first official intervention on the matter came in a letter to Parliament on Christmas Day 1656. Taking 'notice of a judgement lately given by yourselves against one James Nayler', Cromwell assured the Commons that, like them, he did 'detest and abhor the giving or occasioning the least countenance to persons of such opinions and practice'. His main reason for writing was more a concern for the legality of their actions rather than their appropriateness. He merely wished to understand the 'grounds and reasons' on which they had proceeded. Oliver was worried that Parliament's newfound powers of persecution could be employed more widely than just the Quakers. Yet, Cromwell undoubtedly approved of Nayler's punishment. His letter, despite its feigned ignorance of Nayler's fate, came after the savage punishment against the Quaker had already begun. Its purpose was not to bring about a stay of execution pending an inquiry of the legality of the judgement; it was merely a warning against future constitutional excesses.

That the Victorians would hail Cromwell's religious achievements is clearly a skewed construction of his reputation. Seventeenth-century 'liberty of conscience' never really equated with nineteenth-century religious toleration. Had Cromwell lived in Victorian times, he would have been quite alarmed by what he saw. Admittedly, when compared to the rather narrow views of his more puritanical followers, Oliver did allow quite a lot of breathing space for the various Protestant groups that he believed to contain elements of God's truth. Groups such as the Baptists did flourish under his protection and were right to be thankful to his memory. He baulked, however, at the excesses of sects such as the Quakers or at the 'Popish' elements of the Catholic Church. He abhorred 'prelacy', that is, church government by overbearing bishops backed by the enforcement of the 'Anglican' prayer book. There might have been a tacit readmission of Jews into England, but his purpose in allowing this was not intended to tolerate their religious views. In some ways, when it came to religious liberty, Cromwell was 'ahead of his times', but in others he was still a product of that era.

* * *

Cromwell's political vigour also gave him great appeal in Victorian England. His head might rest lifeless, but the dynamism inherent in his reputation invigorated nineteenth-century admirers. Anti-establishment figures looked longingly to the revolution of the 1640s. They praised Cromwell's unwillingness to compromise with Parliaments over constitutional reform. The famous dissolution of the Rump Parliament in April 1653 became an episode enshrined in legend—something to be viewed with admiration and horror in equal amounts. The moment was immortalized in Victorian paintings as a defining point in British history. It was a symbol of one man taking a stand against a corrupt oligarchy. Those championing the Great Reform Act of 1832 found parallels with proposed electoral reforms in the various constitutional documents of the 1640s and 1650s. One contemporary even put out the following advertisement:

> Wanted, a man of the most uncompromising honest and enterprising activity, who will undertake to clear St Stephen's [i.e. the Commons], and the whole country, of a host of vermin who are fattening themselves upon the productions of our poor starving and miserable fellow-countrymen. Any person of the name of Cromwell would be preferred.[17]

Cromwell had become a friend of the radicals, a man of action who did not compromise to get things done. Even if Cromwell's ultimate achievements were not to everybody's taste, the vigour and sincerity with which he pursued his ends was admirable.

He was also a self-made man. The story of Cromwell's lowly upbringing was retold and overemphasized. This humble beginning made Oliver into something of a working-class hero. In 1875, over 2,000 farm labourers gathered at the Cromwell memorial at Naseby to call for better wages, reform of the electoral franchise and agricultural laws. In the same year, 50,000 trade unionists marched through the streets of Manchester in favour of erecting a controversial statue to the Lord Protector.[18] He was portrayed by many as the enemy of nobility, his famous preference for a 'russet-coated captain' over a gentleman struck a chord with the lower echelons of Victorian society. This was a time when meritocracy was gaining over aristocracy. Civil Service examinations, for instance, ensured that men were appointed to serve the State on the basis of skill not background. Cromwell's own meteoric rise from farmer to Lord Protector was something to which many could aspire.

Like Cromwell's religious 'toleration', this Victorian portrayal of the Lord Protector needs qualification. While some aspects of the 'self-made' Cromwell might be true if a little overstated, the notion of his vigour should be carefully scrutinized. Undoubtedly, the story of the dissolution of the 'Rump' or remnant of the Long Parliament shows Cromwell at his most uncompromising. The immediate spur to his actions is often believed to be a proposed Parliamentary bill for the election of future Parliaments. Although the contents of the bill are murky, it would seem that Cromwell believed it would ensure the perpetual sitting of the incumbent Parliament. Appalled by this blatant attempt to override representative elections to secure oligarchic rule, Oliver convened a meeting at his lodgings at Whitehall on the evening of 19 April 1653 to get assurances from MPs that the bill would precede no further. It was a stormy gathering, lasting well into the night. As the MPs wearily departed, a few gave Cromwell assurances that nothing would be done concerning the bill until they had further discussions with him.

The following morning, however, Cromwell was alarmed to hear that preparations for the bill continued apace. He hurried to Westminster and stormed into the house with a file of musketeers. Captured in both the memoirs of Edmund Ludlow and Bulstrode Whitelocke, hardly impartial or untainted accounts, one can see Cromwell at his most manic and forceful. The speech he gave to the Parliament on entering the chamber was littered with abuse at the moral failings of those who sat there. According to Whitelocke, Cromwell:

> In a furious manner bid the speaker leave his chair, told the house that they had sat long enough, unless they had done more good; that some of them were whoremasters, looking then towards Henry Marten and Sir Peter Wentworth:
> The others of them were drunkards, and some corrupt and unjust men, and scandalous to the profession of the gospel, and that it was not fit they should sit as a parliament any longer, and desired them to go away.[19]

According to Ludlow, the MP, Sir Henry Vane, made a stand against Cromwell's hostility, to which Cromwell merely mocked 'O Sir Henry Vane, Sir Henry Vane, the Lord deliver me from Sir Henry Vane'.[20] As the MPs left the chamber bewildered and the Speaker was pulled from his chair, Cromwell 'bid one of his soldiers to take away the fool's bauble the mace'.[21] Created by a military coup in December 1648, the Rump had now been removed by one.

In 1661, Cromwell's head would be set on a spike for killing a king, yet it could be argued his actions in April 1653 were far more daring. Whereas he had taken a back-seat during the regicide, he was at the vanguard of this assault on Parliament. Perhaps it was fitting that Parliament would pass the act for his disinterment in 1660. The Rump, even though it was a purged Parliament, was the last vestige of legitimate authority in the country. The decision to dissolve this assembly was not one taken lightly. In the aftermath of the dissolution, Cromwell would give a number of reasons to justify his actions. Mysteriously, the contents of the Rump's draft 'bill', which had so vexed Cromwell, were never revealed—according to Ludlow, Oliver had 'put it under his cloak' as he left the chamber. Yet his excuses for dissolving the Rump were never predicated on this bill alone. It was the result of over four years of simmering grievances.

Ever since the king's death in 1649, Cromwell and the army had been hoping for much but had received very little. Parliament remained sluggish on the important issues of law reform, reducing taxation and the reformation of manners. While Cromwell was on campaign in Ireland and Scotland from 1649 to 1651, he saw God's divine intervention on the battlefield. His letters are full of praise for God's providences, but they also chided Parliament for their lethargic attitude to building upon God's mercies. Writing to the Speaker of the Commons on 4 September 1650, the day after the Battle of Dunbar, Cromwell was ecstatic:

> Sir, it is in your hands, and by these eminent mercies God puts it more into your hands, to give glory to Him … relieve the oppressed, hear the groans of poor prisoners in England; be pleased to reform the abuses of all professions: and if there be any one that makes many poor to make a few rich, that suits not a Commonwealth.[22]

These were reformist statements that would have appealed to Victorian listeners, but which sadly fell on deaf ears in 1650. The Rump's record on law reform, for instance, was appalling. Despite a number of sensible reforms being devised under a commission headed by the lawyer Matthew Hale, not one of the proposals made it into the statute book. The foot-dragging of lawyer-MPs became notorious. As Cromwell would bitterly reflect, plans to establish a land registry stalled over the filibustering tactics of lawyers: 'we were more than three months [upon it] and could not get over the word "encumbrances".' Picking over every punctilio of draft legislation, the lawyers safeguarded their profession.

More disappointing for Cromwell was the lack of progress made in the way of religious reform. The proposals devised by the Rump were a real hotchpotch. There was the seemingly lenient 'Toleration Act' of September 1650 that repealed the Elizabethan statutes demanding compulsory church attendance. But there was also the confusing 'Blasphemy Act' of August 1650 that condemned the practices and beliefs of deviant sects, especially a group labelled the 'Ranters', while backing it up with only relatively mild punishments. At the other end of the scale was the draconian 'Adultery Act' that proscribed death for those who transgressed. The issue that most raised Cromwell's ire was the debacle over schemes for the propagation of the Gospel. In 1650 the Rump passed legislation to ensure that godly ministers, well-skilled in preaching, were provided for Wales and the northern counties of England—the so-called 'dark corners of the land'. Cromwell lauded this experiment for 'God did kindle a seed there indeed hardly to be paralleled since the primitive times'. The conservative elements of the Rump Parliament, however, disliked the religious radicalism that these commissioners for the propagation of the Gospel seemed to foment. When the original legislation lapsed in April 1653, they did not bother to renew it. Cromwell was furious, condemning 'how signally that

business was trodden underfoot in Parliament to the dis-
countenancing of the honest people'.[23]

Cromwell might have been a 'man of action', but it was
religion that energized those actions. He disliked seeing
God's cause slip while greedy lawyers prevaricated. But it
was also arguably a self-destructive force that drove Cromwell forward. He remained constantly committed to
bringing about reformation for the 'godly' at the same
time as trying to settle the nation at large. His angry dissolution of the Rump Parliament, not to mention the
equally abrupt and hostile end of his two Protectoral Parliaments in 1655 and 1658, merely demonstrated that
Oliver's aims were incompatible with most of the conser-
vative-minded men who sat in Parliament. Cromwell
would praise the Parliamentary constitution of 1657
because it provided both 'for the Liberty of the People of
God and of the nation... I say he sings sweetly that sings a
song of reconciliation betwixt these Interests'.[24] The
problem was that the 'people of God' were only a minority compared to the 'nation' as a whole. To bring about
God's design required Cromwell to ride roughshod over
civil liberties—purging or dissolving Parliaments and
even resorting to the military rule of the Major-Generals.
The painful truth remained that God was no democrat.
In the final analysis, Cromwell would always back the
interests of the godly over the majority.

Victorian perceptions of Cromwell were not too far off
the mark in this sense. He was certainly a man of vigour

and explosive action when his mind was made up. Yet it should be remembered that Cromwell did what he did because he believed it was in the interests of God. Perhaps the greatest facet of Cromwell's personality to be recovered in the Victorian age, especially in Carlyle's rendering of him, was his sincerity. The nineteenth-century emphasis on a corruption-beating, franchise-reforming Cromwell could somewhat secularize his aims and obfuscate the real motives prompting him into action. But, ultimately, the same religious spirit that led him to be identified as a champion of religious liberty would also make him an enemy of rigid constitutionalism.

Less convincing was the early-Victorian working-class, socialist portrayal of Cromwell as an enemy of the nobility. He can hardly be seen engaged in some sort of class war against the upper echelons of society. In reality, he was close friends and political allies with many leading noblemen. He had vigorously opposed the abolition of the House of Lords in 1649 and would arrange for the marriage of two of his daughters to noble families in 1657. As Lord Protector he would use his pseudo-kingly powers to confer two hereditary baronages. He did, however, display an aversion towards political positions descending through the hereditary principal. Under the *Humble Petition and Advice* of 1657, Oliver was obliged to personally nominate members of an 'Other House' or 'upper' chamber to act as a balance to the House of Commons, much in the vein of the defunct House of Lords. Yet, unlike the Lords, the members of this House were not hereditary peers. The names that Cromwell pitched upon are instructive. Only 7 of the 62 named were English peers who would have sat in a traditional House of Lords. Of the rest, there were a conspicuous number of army officers, but there was also a generous helping of conservative 'civilians' and country gentry.

This 'Other House' was designed by Cromwell to check the Commons but also to balance itself. He ensured that all voices were represented—military, civilian and Republican. It was also geographically representative; there were even members from Scotland and Ireland. Cromwell's thinking over this new chamber is best demonstrated in yet another stormy speech at the dissolution of Parliament in February 1658. Its sentiments ring with an attitude to Lord's reform not too dissimilar to Blairite aspirations:

> It was granted I should name another House. I named it
> of men that shall meet you wheresoever you go, and shake
> hands with you; and tell you it is not Titles, nor Lords,
> nor Party that they value, but a Christian and an English
> Interest! Men of your own rank and quality, who will not
> only be a balance unto you, but [a balance] to themselves.[25]

Cromwell did not want to destroy nobility, but he did not necessarily believe that it should have a monopoly over government. In this way, the Victorian middle-class admiration of Cromwell as an advocate for meritocracy has some truth in it.

* * *

The rising tide of Cromwellianism in the Victorian era was thus a product of a distorted reading of Oliver's reputation. His moral fortitude, religious toleration, political boldness and sincere piety all endeared Cromwell to nineteen-century audiences. In this context, it was only natural that both the media and public alike took a keen interest in Cromwell's head. Unlike eighteenth-century observers who looked upon the head more as a grisly artefact, it had now become a meaningful object once again. It was admired more because of the man it represented than for its gruesome features. When Josiah Wilkinson purchased the head in 1815 he would have been unaware of the cult that would grow around Cromwell by the 1890s. In the late nineteenth century his grandson, Horace Wilkinson, would come to lament the interest that the head generated. What would have been a blessing for the publicity-hungry Cranch and the Hughes brothers in 1799, had become a curse for Wilkinson a century later. Locked away in its oak box and stored safely under Wilkinson's bed, Cromwell's head remained extremely 'private' in a climate that increasingly demanded 'public' recognition of the great man.

It was this demand for public commemoration that would lead to the erection of an iconic statue of Cromwell in his tercentenary year. Stood in a sunken green outside Parliament, the bronze statue still gazes out broodingly on thousands of tourists today. Designed by Sir Hamo Thornycroft, the Cromwell statue is everything that the Victorians wanted the Lord Protector to be. There is a vigour, not to mention a menace, about the way he grasps his sword in front of the Houses of Parliament. He is dressed in the garb of a soldier rather than a civilian. At the same time, in his left hand, he clutches a Bible: a symbol of his piety, but the catalyst for so many of his most contentious actions.

Yet why should Cromwell find himself memorialized outside Parliament? A man who had notoriously used force against elected assemblies on numerous occasions could hardly be figured the father of modern Parliamentary liberties. Indeed, the statue itself was not without controversy. The fact it is consigned to an anonymous green, rather than a prominent position within Westminster, is highly suggestive. The epitaph at its base merely reads: 'Oliver Cromwell, 1599–1658', thereby glossing over the legitimacy of his title of 'Lord Protector'. Even with the growing Victorian cult of Cromwell, he was still a controversial figure. The story of the Thornycroft statue serves as a microcosm of this contested reputation.

The statue was the necessary answer to those who bewailed the paucity of tributes to Cromwell. It will be remembered that this lack of commemoration astounded the American journalist William Breed as he passed through London *en route* to conduct his 'interview' with Wilkinson's head in 1884.[26] The one-time Liberal Prime Minister, Lord Rosebery, also shared his concerns. His attempts to get Parliament to accept the building of the Cromwell statue would end up bringing down his government. As much as 'popular' demand might be behind Cromwell, there were still groups who were not so predisposed to revere his memory.

The opportunity to erect a statue at Westminster arose in the aftermath of the great fire of 1834 that destroyed the old Parliamentary buildings. As part of the rebuilding programme, it was intended to commemorate notable figures of Parliament's past in paintings, statues and stained glass. By the 1840s an ambitious scheme was devised to commemorate all English monarchs in statue form within the new building. Yet, as the newspapers were quick to point out, where would this leave Cromwell? Should he be allowed to take his place among the pantheon of kings? Some argued it was fitting reparation for the detestable acts committed on his body in the Restoration era. Others were more circumspect. They pondered whether Cromwell really would have welcomed commemoration among the kings. He was not exactly favourable towards monarchy in his own lifetime. It was a well-argued point, displaying more sensitivity to what Cromwell would have wanted than those who had crudely appropriated his image for the pompous monarchical funeral of 1658. In the end all this bickering was to no avail. The commission in charge of the arts project at the new Westminster declined to consider commemorating Cromwell among England's monarchy. Thereafter, agitation for a statue to Cromwell at Westminster came in intermittent drifts. Flaring up during the bicentenary year of Cromwell's death, 1858, it then died down again until the early 1870s. It was in the dying years of the nineteenth century, however, that the plan would finally come to fruition.

By the mid 1890s, Lord Rosebery was in a quandary. As Liberal Party leader and the incumbent Prime Minister he was struggling to keep together the disparate groups on which his power rested. Rosebery admired Cromwell because of his dynamic spirit and the ruthless effectiveness with which he was able to maintain political control; qualities that the Prime Minister was sorely lacking. Rosebery's attraction to Cromwell was also a matter of politics. A major part of the Liberal Party's following derived from the Nonconformists. Capitalizing on the Cromwell cult at the end of the century, Rosebery's plan to erect a statue to Cromwell was designed to win over the support of those Nonconformists who had misgivings about the new Prime Minister. They had reason to be concerned; treading in the footsteps of Gladstone, Rosebery had a hard act to follow. His self-professed love for horse racing alarmed more sober spirits. Indeed, there is a delicious irony about Rosebery erecting a statue to the man who had famously ordered the banning of race meetings.

Nevertheless, Rosebery's commitment to the Cromwell statue was intended to be an appeal to Nonconformist sensibilities as well as the public at large.

Getting Parliament to agree to the building of the statue proved more difficult than Rosebery could have imagined. Popular support might be on his side, but establishment figures proved obstinate. Cabinet meetings were spent in fierce debate over the proposals. Queen Victoria was reputedly not amused by Rosebery's scheme. The Prime Minister was forced to change his plans. He even admitted to his colleagues, in rather understated terms, that Cromwell was not really 'a great parliamentarian in the strict sense'. In the end, Rosebery managed to get what he wanted, albeit the statue was not to stand in Westminster, but was consigned to an obscure sunken green outside the building.

Even then, one final hurdle stood in Rosebery's way. When, in June 1895, the Commons were asked to provide the money for the Cromwell statue, Irish Nationalists sitting in the House launched a bitter tirade. It was a worrying moment for Rosebery given that his ministry depended on Irish votes. By trying to please the Nonconformists, Rosebery had effectively committed political suicide with the Irish Nationalists. The Irish contingent made impassioned speeches to the chamber, reminding them of the atrocities committed by Cromwell in their home country. It was a forceful argument and one that continues to blight Oliver's reputation to the present day.[27] The government had to back down; Rosebery's administration collapsed shortly afterwards.

Unruffled by this catastrophic rebuff, Rosebery decided that the project should go on, even if he had to fund it out of his own pocket. Hearing of Rosebery's defeat, the *London Chronicle* called for public subscriptions to fund a monument to Cromwell. Within 24 hours they had received pledges for all the money that was required. Support for Cromwell was definitely strong. The Pittsburg historian Samuel Church, the same man who was so keen to have Cromwell's head examined in 1895, was convinced that despite some staunch opposition, the groundswell of pro-Cromwellian feeling would win the day. Although 'the dominant Tory sentiment among the upper classes' had kept Cromwell 'buried under a mountain of prejudice until recently', it was Church's belief that 'There is now a reaction going on which should reach its full force and international strength in 1899... I believe that that will be the day of Oliver Cromwell's final vindication, when he will come into his own to the good opinion of mankind'.[28] These were prescient words. Although some opposition lingered, Rosebery stumped up the cash for the statue and it was finally erected in Cromwell's tercentenary year—just as Church predicted. A number of delaying tactics in Parliament, not to mention a petition against the statue, meant that the unveiling did not take place on Cromwell's birthday (25 April) or on the day of his death (3 September). Instead, to avoid any further controversy, it occurred on a cold November's morning at half past seven in front of a conspicuously small crowd. Like the burial of Cromwell's head 60 years later, it was a low-key affair but it marked an important phase in the commemoration of Oliver Cromwell. Unthinkable a century earlier, Oliver had finally gained public recognition, even acceptance, if not complete admiration.

* * *

The Victorian age did a lot to enhance Oliver Cromwell's reputation. Not always an accurate portrayal of the man in life, it was certainly more sympathetic than at any time since his death. Cromwell, thanks to numerous statues and other artworks, became perhaps the most recognized historical figure in Britain. Carlyle's work ensured that more and more people came to understand Oliver through his own words, rather than the bitter invective of his detractors. It certainly was the apogee of Cromwellianism. But it was also a false dawn. The image was never an accurate or convincing one. By the middle of the twentieth century few would be willing to partake in the unconditional hero-worship of the Victorians. Indeed, by the 1930s, Cromwell was hijacked by the fascist movements across Europe. Adolf Hitler, for instance, justified his seizure of power in 1933 in an interview in the *New York Times* by drawing parallels with Cromwell's vigorous dissolution of Parliament. The Victorian emphasis on Cromwellian 'vigour' and 'action' had been taken to new extremes. The formulation of Cromwell as 'dictator' persisted well into the second half of the twentieth century. Cromwell had appealed to Victorian society because certain facets of his character commended themselves to the concerns of that age. As one historian would emphatically state in 1897, Cromwell was the 'national hero of the nineteenth century'. Once that generation passed, so did its highly favourable construction of Cromwell.

Yet, while Cromwell's image became widely known and revered at the latter end of the nineteenth century, his head remained conspicuously anonymous. In part, this was due to lingering doubts about its authenticity. Although Cromwell's face was recognizable to everybody, most notably in Thornycroft's iconic statue, the dulled, withered features of his real head left it open to doubt. Despite repeated calls in the media for the head to be properly scrutinized, Wilkinson remained unmoved. Indeed, while the growing cult of Cromwell might have raised interest in his head, it was advances in science that would allow the head to be examined in a different light. The nineteenth century saw the development of X-rays, photography and other aspects of 'forensic' science that made it possible to get closer to finding the 'real' head of Oliver Cromwell. Unlike artistic representations of Cromwell, it was not enough to glance at the outward features of the head to prove it was genuine. Rigorous scientific investigation was required, and frequently demanded. It would be another 30 years, however, before the head was finally offered up for testing.

Despite the Victorian cult of Cromwell, the head itself never really took centre stage in the commemorations around his tercentenary year. Yet that did not stop people taking a great deal of interest in the object. Men such as Samuel Church had envisioned Cromwell's head, once proven genuine, to be interred under a magnificent bronze monument to the Lord Protector such as that at Westminster. Public feeling was that Cromwell's head belonged to the 'public' and deserved a decent, honourable burial. It was not to be. In emulation of Cromwell's own life for his first 40 years, his head continued living in rural obscurity with the Wilkinson family.

Perhaps this is what Cromwell himself would have wanted. Throughout his time in power he had complained of his burdens; just like Gideon he had longed to retire to the anonymity of the country once the fighting was over. Cromwell never sought fame or fortune for himself or his family, nor did he profess himself to be a hero. That his surviving mortal remains were distanced from the charade of 1899 is therefore only fitting.

* VI *
The Many 'Heads' of Cromwell

IT IS NOW 350 years since that fateful stormy afternoon of 3 September 1658. Yet even after the Lord Protector drew his final breath, he continued to exert his presence on the world he left behind. His paradoxical character and his remarkable achievements could still excite, engage, fascinate and infuriate people long after his death. In many ways the story of Cromwell's head and his posthumous immortality, even infamy, are closely intertwined. The fortunes of Cromwell's head perfectly reflect attitudes towards him through the generations. From post-Restoration desecration to early eighteenth-century obscurity, from late Victorian exaltation to twentieth-century examination, both Cromwell's head and reputation have had a rollercoaster of a ride.

The vile acts carried out on the bodies of Cromwell, Ireton and Bradshaw in January 1661 brought the late Lord Protector back into the public imagination. While the bloodthirsty butchery of the gallows consigned his body to the oblivion of the common pit, it also set his head on its epic journey. The notoriety of a traitor's pole ensured that Cromwell's reputation would remain blackened for quite some time, but it helped people to remember him. By necessity, the disinterring of Cromwell and the continued afterlife of his head also aided the resurrection of interest in the man behind the head. Even while Charles I and Charles II lay dead and their bodies turned to dust, their arch-enemy, Cromwell, would live on both in body and memory. Through the ages, the visitors who attended the grisly peep-shows, such as Du Puy's museum, Samuel Russell's market stall, Cranch's Bond Street exhibition or Wilkinson's Victorian parlour were invited to gaze upon this unique relic and to think of its erstwhile owner (see plate 24). As time went on, the story behind the head fascinated just as much as the head itself.

Perhaps the most intriguing, not to mention consistent, theme in the story of Cromwell's head is that of the attempts to conclusively prove it was genuine. The motives for those who wanted to prove the head's authenticity varied. For some it was purely down to greed; James Cox, John Cranch and the Hughes brothers all sought to verify the head's provenance in order to make money from it. For others it was a matter of antiquarian or scientific curiosity; from the musings of the curator of the Ashmolean Museum and the sympathetic examination of the Royal Archaeological Institute through to the rigorous probing of Morant and Pearson in the early twentieth century. Behind all these attempts, however, was a consistent climate of scepticism. Many who viewed the head doubted what they saw. Like Cromwell in life, it was not enough to take him at face value.

Ironically, it was Cromwell himself who aided the process of finding his real head. Cromwell's self-effacing style, embodied in his profession to be painted 'warts and all', meant that many 'accurate' images of the Lord Protector were made recording the fine detail of his facial features. The numerous portraits, busts and masks of Cromwell's head were a dream for those wishing to carry out biometrical analysis on his real head. Measurements were taken, statistical data collated and averages calculated. The telltale wart of Cromwell's portraiture matched perfectly with the depression above the right eye of the mummified head. By closely examining the honest, plain way Cromwell had wished to be portrayed in life, scientists were able to conclusively identify Horace Wilkinson's gruesome possession to be genuine.

If only the same process could be used to find the 'real' man behind the head. As we have seen, Cromwell's reputation both in life and death was hardly clear-cut. His self-styled 'plain' image was never as simple as Cromwell would have us believe. Possibly a mark of hubris or careful self-styling, Cromwell's excessively godly demeanour actually concealed his real character. He was never really that one-dimensional. A keen lover of music, and attending (in seventeenth-century terms) some rather wild parties, Cromwell could joke, drink and frolic with the best of them. Moreover, in death, Cromwell became even more contested. Blurred in his own lifetime, in subsequent ages Cromwell's reputation became, at times, distorted out of all recognition. Over time, different 'layers' of reputation have formed with each historical generation. Yet, even as these various posthumous renderings of Oliver are unpicked, he remains an enigma. He was a curious compound of contradictory characteristics. In reality, Cromwell had not one but many 'heads'.

On the one side Cromwell was an unassuming, conservative gentleman. Born into the lower gentry, he briefly slipped to the position of a yeoman farmer before recovering his status via a well-timed family death. He was both an overbearing and loving father. He ensured that all his children secured marriages that were lucrative in both financial and spiritual terms. Even when he took hold of the reigns of power after 1653, Oliver continued to look after family life. In politics, Cromwell often displayed a streak of conservatism that was disconcerting to men of more radical opinions. It can explain why he dragged his feet for so long on the issue of regicide and why he never completely abandoned hope of settling the nation on a constitutional basis backed by Parliament. It was this side of Cromwell that those who offered him the Crown in 1657 hoped to draw out. Realizing an inherent yearning in Cromwell to return to 'known ways', they hoped that he would join with them in rebuilding the Ancient Constitution of King, Lords and Commons. Yet, even if Cromwell was a product of the lesser gentry, his experiences and allegiances from the early 1640s onwards meant that he could never really settle with the conservatives. Within the mild-mannered Dr Jekyll lurked a fiery, often radical, Mr Hyde.

Arguably, it is Cromwell's zealous nature that accounts for his endearing quality. It can explain why the quiet man of the Cambridgeshire fens could transform into the brilliant, at times ruthless, military commander of the Civil Wars. Ultimately, Cromwell was a man of God. It was God, both through His Word, laid down in the Bible, and through His actions, as demonstrated by innumerable Providences, which drove Cromwell forward. Ever since his 'conversion' in the 1630s, Cromwell looked to God to rationalize the numerous crises through which he travelled. Oliver's fiery puritanical spirit often jostled with, and more often than not won over, his conservative instincts. It led him to some of his most commendable actions—such as the refusal of the Crown. But it also accounts for the more controversial episodes of his life. It drove him to kill the king and to expel the self-serving Rump Parliament. His heartfelt belief to be bringing about God's work also helped to counter later accusations of hypocrisy. Even if his actions were not commended, the motives behind them were sincere.

Yet this intensely godly side to Cromwell has also led

to him being demonized by some. There was a fine line between believing to act in God's best interest and using this as a justification to back a ruthless dictatorship. Indeed, it was arguably an overconfidence in divine backing that led Cromwell to his most controversial, most hotly debated and, ultimately, his most detestable act—the massacres in Ireland. Given the subsequent impact that the storming of Drogheda and Wexford have had on Oliver's reputation, they remain too big a blight on his copybook to be ignored.

Cromwell was incensed with the Irish Catholics. In 1641 they had fomented a rebellion against Protestant settlers that had led to the massacre of thousands. The ferocious butchery that followed Cromwell's storming of the town of Drogheda on 11 September 1649, in which both soldiers and civilians lost their lives, was explained away as divinely ordained revenge for 1641. In a letter to the Speaker of the House of Commons a few days later, Oliver would exclaim that this was:

> A righteous judgement of God upon these barbarous wretches, who have imbrued their hands in so much innocent blood; and that it will tend to prevent the effusion of blood for the future, which are the satisfactory grounds to such actions, which otherwise cannot but work remorse and regret... God alone have all the glory.[1]

There have been numerous apologies made for Cromwell's actions. The severity with which Cromwell ordered the garrison to be subdued was on a par with comparable savagery during the Thirty Years War on the Continent. Fierce debate continues over whether the Royalist garrison commander had both been offered and accepted surrender. Were the killings in the heat of battle or merely in cold blood? Were there significant civilian causalities? It seems certain that those defending Drogheda were actually a mixture of English Royalists, Irish Protestants and Catholics, thus making Cromwell's excuse of subduing the 'barbarous wretches' of 1641 somewhat flimsy.

Of course, much of the historical debate on this episode has been coloured by political and nationalist passions. Yet this is the point. Cromwell's extreme godliness has left him open, whether rightly or wrongly, to posthumous demonization. His piety might have led to him being exalted to almost saint-like status by Victorian Nonconformists, but it could also reveal a less than endearing side to the Lord Protector. At times it could drive him to monstrous extremes. It led to an almost nihilistic overconfidence in his abilities and actions. His belief that the unrestrained savagery at Drogheda in September 1649, and Wexford a month later, would 'prevent the effusion of blood' in the future was misplaced. This early-modern 'shock and awe' tactic merely solidified Irish opposition against Cromwell and his army. Waterford and Duncannon would both successfully repel the Parliamentary onslaught later that year. The siege of Clonmel in May 1650 would see Oliver suffer one of his greatest setbacks as a military commander: losing in excess of 2,000 men. More importantly, Cromwell's actions in Ireland have helped to colour Anglo-Irish relations to the present day. His savagery has become a powerful metaphor for the treatment by the English of the indigenous population. As one early twentieth-century commentator remarked of Cromwell's time in Ireland, 'it was a tragic necessity that the Irish should remember it; but it was far more tragic that the English forgot it'.[2]

It was this split personality, almost schizophrenic at times, that has continued to fascinate. He was both a low-born country gentleman and a pseudo-monarchical head of state; a loving family man and a savage Parliamentary general; a dour puritan and a keen patron of the arts. In his head, he was a political conservative but in his heart lurked a fiery religious spirit. That Cromwell has continued to spark interest through the ages is down to the fact that his reputation and character are so malleable. Each generation has been able to take or ignore certain facets for their own ends. For those living through the Restoration, the fire-breathing puritanical tyrant came to the fore; for the admiring Victorians it was Cromwell's piety, sincerity and vigour that were emphasized. As Cromwell's head continued on its amazing journey, it was the changeable nature of his reputation that provided the fuel for its travels. Just as scholars came to argue over the authenticity of the head, they also debated the genuineness of the man behind the head. Indeed, the most consistent facet of Cromwell's reputation throughout the ages was its ability to divide opinion.

* * *

So what of Cromwell today? Oliver's head has now been buried for over 40 years in the tranquil surroundings of Sidney Sussex, Cambridge. Kept quiet until after the interment ceremony, the college's prized possession is still famous enough to draw a modest crowd. Although the head would never take its place under some grand Victorian monument to the Lord Protector, the antechapel of Sidney Sussex has become something of a Cromwellian shrine. Now and again, a tourist can be seen peering curiously into the college chapel. Not quite the grand catafalque erected in Westminster Abbey in 1658, the austerity of the head's surroundings are perhaps more in keeping with the man commemorated there. After taking a snapshot of the simple plaque that announces the burial, many pause to ponder the whereabouts of the head. That, however, remains a secret.

Yet even with Cromwell's head buried, he is not forgotten. Ever since his death in 1658, Cromwell has had the uncanny ability to live on. He still generates enough interest to be immortalized in today's 'popular culture'. He has captured the imagination of poets, novelists and dramatists. He has even made it onto the big screen including the Hammer Horror film *Witchfinder General* (1968) and the more recent, if not equally far-fetched, *To*

Kill a King (2002). Most memorable, however, is the epic film *Cromwell* (1970), with Alec Guinness cast brilliantly as the hopeless Charles I and the Irish actor Richard Harris inexplicably playing the leading role. Given Cromwell's love of music, not to mention his idiosyncratic sense of humour, one wonders how much he might have enjoyed Monty Python's surprisingly accurate rendering of his life in prose set to a piece by Chopin. Mockery aside, Oliver has also appeared on TV in numerous dramatizations, not to mention a plethora of historical documentaries of varying quality. Hundreds of biographies, weighing up his reputation and achievements, have been published since the time of Carlyle through to the present day—of which this is yet another! On the whole, their conclusions are balanced—never totally hostile, nor altogether laudatory.

Building on the Victorian cult of Cromwell, commemoration of the Lord Protector has continued to abound. There are more than 250 roads in Britain bearing his name—perhaps more than any other figure in English history. Winston Churchill admired the man so much that he tried to convince King George V to name a battleship after Cromwell with predictable results. Yet, during the Second World War, Churchill was more successful in getting George VI to agree to name a class of cruiser tank after the great Parliamentarian general. In 1951, British Rail named a steam locomotive after him; it would have the notable distinction of hauling the final steam passenger train in Britain in 1968. Today there are hundreds of web-sites that seek to commemorate Cromwell's memory—good or bad. There is also the Cromwell Association, established in 1935 by the Liberal politician Isaac Foot to promote the understanding of both Oliver and his times. Even today, the Association continues to thrive with a healthy membership. Every 3 September, or 'Cromwell Day' as it has become known, members meet under the statue of Thornycroft outside Westminster to pay their respects to the Lord Protector. In 1962 the old grammar school in Huntingdon, in which Thomas Beard had taught the young Oliver Cromwell, was converted into a museum crammed full of Cromwellian curiosities—including death masks, portraits and even Cromwell's hat!

That is not to say that Cromwell has had it all his own way in recent years. Cromwell's reputation in Ireland remains in the doldrums. The opposition to Lord Rosebery's proposals to erect the Cromwell statue in 1895 was just one example of this. In 2000, plans to display Cromwell's death mask in a local museum at Drogheda provoked a fresh wave of uproar. Over 350 years since the atrocities committed there, many of the local inhabitants, including the deputy mayor, were incensed by the insensitivity of such an exhibit. At Durham University, a storm was raised when a plan was revealed to name one of its colleges after the Lord Protector—many rather ungratefully forgetting that it was the Lord Protector who had first granted the institution university status. In 1999,

Cromwell's quatercentenary year, Catholics boycotted celebrations in the Lord Protector's home town of Huntingdon. Cromwell might continue to grab the headlines, but it has not always been in a favourable light.

Perhaps the most fascinating testimony to the continued interest in Cromwell is the 'Greatest Britons' poll that ran on BBC television at the start of the new millennium. Although some more recent 'celebrities' crept into the list, voted for by the public, Oliver Cromwell made it into the top ten—securing over 45,000 votes. He came higher than any monarch of England, save Queen Elizabeth I, demonstrating that many still do care about the achievements and actions of Cromwell. Even 350 years after his death, people believe that he made a significant impact on the history of the British Isles. He continues to be a figure worth remembering.

* * *

Cromwell's head may have been given its low-key burial in March 1960, but one should not see this as an end to the story. Although the journey of Cromwell's head was a fascinating and often bizarre one, it was never really the head that was the most important aspect of the whole affair. The really remarkable thing was the preservation of Cromwell's memory and the different shades of opinion that it could evoke. Whether rightly or wrongly, Cromwell has been maligned and praised in equal measure throughout the ages. He continues to divide opinion and that seems unlikely to change anytime soon. Today, attitudes are certainly more favourable than in 1661, yet not quite as forgiving as they were in 1899. Although the Cromwellian 'bogeyman' figure of folklore continues to persist, twenty-first-century attitudes to Cromwell remain fairly balanced. Maybe all this will change as future generations look on him with fresh eyes. Cromwell's head may now rest in peace at Sidney Sussex College, but his enigmatic presence will cast a shadow into this millennium and beyond. The reports at Oliver's death were highly prescient in that respect: having decided to refuse the earthly crown in life, Cromwell has almost certainly received 'the crown of everlasting life'.[3]

Notes on the Text

Introduction

1 British Library, Additional
MS. 43724 fo. 45.

2 N. PENNY (ed.), *The Journal
of George Fox* (London,
1924), p.173.

3 T. BIRCH (ed.), *A Collection
of State Papers of John Thurloe*
(7 vols., London, 1742), vii,
pp.354–6.

4 *Ibid.*, vii, pp.363–4.

5 *Ibid.*, vii, p.369.

6 *Ibid.*, vii, pp.372–3.

7 *Ibid.*, vii, p.367.

8 *The Publick Intelligencer*, 141,
pp.794–6.

9 *Calender of State Papers,
Venetian 1657–9*, p.248.

10 P. GAUNT, (ed.), *The
Correspondence of Henry
Cromwell, 1655–1659: British
Library Lansdowne Manu-
scripts*, Camden Society,
5th series, xxxi (2007),
p.410.

11 *The Publick Intelligencer*,
142, p.816; 147, p.912.

12. *Ibid.*, 148, pp.917–19.

13 *The True Manner of the most
Magnificent Conveyance of his
Highnesse Effigies* (London,
1658), p.8.

14 M.M. VERNEY, *Memoirs of
the Verney Family* (4 vols.,
London, 1925), ii, p.130.

15 *The Publick Intelligencer*, 152,
p.7.

16 C.H. FIRTH (ed.), *Memoirs
of Edmund Ludlow* (2 vols,
Oxford, 1894), ii, pp.47–8.

17 A. COWLEY, *A Vision,
Concerning the late Pretended
Highnesse Cromwell*
(London, 1661) p.2.

18 E. BURROUGH, *A Testimony
Against a Great Idolatry*
(London, 1658) p.2.

19 The National Archives,
SP18/183, fo. 191v.

20 *The Publick Intelligencer*, 152,
pp.21–3.

21 BURROUGH, p.5.

22 G. WITHER, *Salt upon Salt*
(London, 1659) p.18.

23 H. FLETCHER, *The Perfect
Politician Or, A Full View of
the Life and Action... Of*

O. Cromwell (London, 1660) p.343; *The Publick Intelligencer*, 152, pp.21–3; S. CARRINGTON, *History of the Life and Death of His most Serene Highness*, pp.237–40.

24 C.H. FIRTH (ed.), *The Clarke Papers* (4 vols., Camden Society, 1891–1901), iii, p.168.

25 *True Manner*, p.12; *The Publick Intelligencer*, 152, p.7 (16 Nov.).

26 TNA, SP18/183, fo. 191.

27 TNA, SP18/183, fo. 190.

28 A full list of the processional order is provided in the British Library, Lansdowne MS 95, fos. 31–45.

29 *Ludlow*, ii, pp.47–8.

30 Bodleian Library, MS Clarendon 59 fos. 238–9.

31 E.S. BEER (ed.), *Diary of John Evelyn* (6 vols., Oxford, 1955), iii, p.224.

32 M. GUIZOT, *History of Richard Cromwell and the Restoration of Charles II*, A. SCOBLE, trans. (2 vols., London, 1856), i, pp.266–70; *CSP Venetian, 1657–9*, pp.268–9.

33 GUIZOT, *Richard Cromwell*, i, pp.266–70.

34 COWLEY, pp.2–3.

35 *A Collection of Several Passages concerning his late Highnesse Oliver Cromwell* (London, 1659), pp.12–13.

Chapter I

1 *Mercurius Publicus* (24–31 Jan. 1661), p.64; *The Diary of John Evelyn*, 30 Jan. 1661; J. HEATH, *Flagellum* (London, 1663), p.211.

2 Although Sainthill's MS is now missing, a transcription is given in T.R. NASH (ed.) *Butler's Hudibras*, (3 vols., London, 1793), III, pp.379–80.

3 Bodleian Library, Rawlinson MS A 315, fos. 234–8.

4 TNA, SP 77/33 fo. 146 (Nicholas to Sir H. de Vic, 1 Feb. 1661).

5 *CSP 1660–1*, 8 February 1661 (Nicholas to Sir William Curtis). Original in TNA, SP 29/30 fo. 52 (written in French).

6 Evelyn misdates the funeral as 22 November; it should be 23 November 1658.

7 Mundy says '4 or 5 hours', Bod. Lib. Rawlinson MS A 315, fos. 234–8; Evelyn notes that the bodies were hanged

until 6pm, but this seems unlikely given that most other accounts say that the time of the beheading was sunset.

8 *Hudibras*, III, pp.379–80.

9 *Mercurius Publicus* (31 Jan–7 Feb 1661), p.80.

10 *CSP Venetian 1659–61*, p.162.

11 *Mercurius Publicus* (May 10–17 1660); See also the wording of the Act of Attainder in *Statutes of the Realm*, vol. v, pp.288–90.

12 *State Trials*, vol. v, p.1265.

13 Quoted in C.V. WEDGWOOD, *The Trial of Charles I* (London, 2001), p.223.

14 *Old Parliamentary History*.

15 TNA, SP 29/23 fo. 70 (10 Dec. 1660).

16 J.W. WILLIS BUND (ed.), *The Diary of Henry Town-shend* (London, 1915), pp.64–5.

17 Most would be likewise exhumed during this period and transferred to nearby St. Margaret's or a common pit. Cromwell's daughter, Elizabeth Claypole, is believed to have evaded the graverobbers and still lies within the chapel to this day.

18 *Weekly Post*, 31 May–7 June 1659.

19 M. NOBLE, *Memoirs of the Protectoral House of Cromwell*, (2 vols., London, 1787), i, pp.288–91.

20 W.L. SACHSE (ed.), *The Diurnal of Thomas Rugge, 1659–1661* (Camden Society, 1961) p.143.

21 TNA, PRO 31/17/33, p.41 (Transcription of the Order Book of the Privy Council — 14 Sept. 1658).

22 The 'gold' plaque still survives today at the Museum of London.

23 *Mercurius Publicus* (24–31 Jan. 1661), p.64.

24 TNA, PRO 31/17/33, pp.5–6.

25 BATE, *Elenchus Motuum*, (London, 1685), p.236. This is an English translation of an earlier Latin text from the 1660s.

26 GUIZOT, *Richard Cromwell*, i, p.260; *Clarke Papers*, iii, pp.167–8; VERNEY, *Memoirs of the Verney Family*, iii, p.422.

27 J. BANKS, *A Short Critical Review of the Life of Oliver Cromwell* (London, 1740), p.212; NOBLE, i, pp.288–91. The story supposedly comes from Colonel Barkstead, Lieutenant of the Tower of London during the Protectorate.

28 PEPYS, Samuel *Diary*, 13 October 1664.

29 This is the view of F.J. VARLEY in *Oliver Cromwell's Latter End* (London, 1939), pp.53–8.

30 J. PRESTWICH, *Respublica* (London, 1787), p.149. This obelisk no longer exists. A more recent proponent of this ridiculous theory is Prof. H.F. McMains in his *The Death of Oliver Cromwell* (Kentucky, 2000), pp. 59–78. Which claims, incredibly, that Milton and Marvell arranged for the Holborn substitution.

31 A. SMITH, 'The Image of Cromwell in Folklore and Tradition', *Folklore*, 79 (1968), pp.37–8.

32 J.D. DURNOVARIAE, *Short Meditations on the Life and Death of Oliver Cromwell*, p.7.

33 SACHSE, *Diurnal*, p.114.

34 PEPYS, *Diary*, 4 Dec. 1660.

35 Quoted in K. PEARSON and G. MORANT, 'The Wilkinson Head of Oliver Cromwell', *Biometrika*, 26 (1934), p.57.

36 *London Gazette*, 20 June 1684.

37 PEARSON and MORANT, p.12.

38 The original of this account, written by Josiah Henry Wilkinson in 1827, is kept in the archives of Sidney Sussex.

39 Uffenbach's account is quoted in PEARSON and MORANT, pp.22–3. Many thanks to Paul Howard for help with the German translation.

Chapter II

1 From an account by Josiah Wilkinson written in 1827, now in the possession of Sidney Sussex College.

2 This document still survives in the archives of Sidney Sussex College.

3 Quoted in PEARSON and MORANT, p.12.

4 The draft handbill, written by Cranch, is preserved at Sidney Sussex.

5 It is interesting to note that Cranch's illustration of the head on the front cover of this brochure is almost identical to the appearance of the head in 1960.

6 NOBLE, i, p.291.

7 H. HOWARTH, *The Embalmed Head of Oliver Cromwell* (London, 1911),

pp.14–15; Brit. Lib., Add. MS 6306, fo. 84.

8 Quoted in HOWARTH, pp.14–15.

9 Quoted in MORANT and PEARSON, p.25.

10 Josiah Wilkinson's letters and documents concerning the head, as well as the Cranch Papers, survive in the archives of Sidney Sussex College.

11 *Notes and Queries*, Series. X, Vol. XI (1849), p.453.

12 HOWARTH, p.10.

13 See HOWARTH for the full report of the Royal Archaeological Institute.

14 See article by D. ROYSTON BOOTH in *The Daily Telegraph*, 26/10/1962.

Chapter III

1 T. CARLYLE, *The Letters and Speeches of Oliver Cromwell*, ed. S.C. Lomas (3 vols., London, 1904), ii, p.541.

2 *Ibid.*, iii, p.121.

3 B. WHITELOCKE, *Memorials of the English Affairs* (4 vols., Oxford, 1853), ii, p.471.

4 Quoted in S.R. GARDINER, *History of the Great Civil War* (4 vols., London, 1889), iii, pp.271–2.

5 Quoted in GARDINER, *Civil War*, iii, p.341.

6 The passage is from JOHN WILDMAN's *Putney Projects*, printed in A.S.P. WOODHOUSE, *Puritanism and Liberty* (Dent, 1938) pp.426–8.

7 D.M. WOLFE, *Leveller Manifestoes* (London, 1944), pp.198–221.

8 *Clarke Papers*, i, pp.228, 255, 283–4, 300–301, 376–7, 369–83.

9 The account of the Windsor prayer meeting comes from WILLIAM ALLEN's later published account, *A Faithful Memorial of that Remarkable Meeting ... at Windsor Castle* (London, 1659). Interestingly, this is the same biblical reference made by Fleetwood shortly before Oliver's death (see Introduction).

10 W.C. ABBOTT, *The Writings and Speeches of Oliver Cromwell* (4 vols., Oxford, 1989) i, p.691.

11 CARLYLE, i, p.399.

12 *Ludlow*, i, p.211.

13 This attempt is mentioned in WHITELOCKE, *Memorials*, ii, p.477.

14 S.R. GARDINER (ed.), *The Constitutional Documents of*

the Puritan Revolution, 1625–60, (3rd edn., Oxford, 1906), p.374.

15 TNA, SP16/517 fos. 16v–17r. (Account of Trial of Charles I, 20 Jan. 1649).

16 Bod. Lib., Clarendon MS 54, fos. 108–116v.

17 J.T. RUTT (ed.), *The Diary of Thomas Burton Esq.*, (4 vols., London, 1828), i, pp.382–5.

18 GARDINER *Constitutional Documents*, p.458.

19 CARLYLE, iii, pp.26–7.

20 *Ibid.*, iii, pp.29–33.

21 *Monarchy Asserted* (London, 1660), p.11.

22 *Monarchy Asserted*, p.19.

23 CARLYLE, iii, p.54.

24 *Ibid.*, iii, pp.70–71.

25 J. NICKOLLS (ed.), *Original Letters and Papers of State … addressed to Oliver Cromwell* (London, 1743), pp.141–2.

26 CARLYLE, iii, p.189 (Cromwell to Parliament, 4 Feb. 1658).

27 BURROUGH, pp.3–4.

Chapter IV

1 Brit. Lib., Additional MS 23,069. This anecdote was first recorded in the eighteenth century.

2 J. MORRILL, 'The Making of Oliver Cromwell' in Morrill (ed.), *Oliver Cromwell and the English Revolution* (Longman, 1990), p.28.

3 HEATH, p.8.

4 CARLYLE, i, pp.89–90.

5 See Chapter III.

6 MORRILL 'The Making of Oliver Cromwell', pp.43–5.

7 CARLYLE, i, p.89.

8 J.P. KENYON (ed.), *The Stuart Constitution* (2nd ed., Cambridge, 1986), pp.322–4.

9 ABBOTT, i, p.256.

10 P. WARWICK, *Memoirs* (Edinburgh, 1813), pp.273–5.

11 *Diary of John Evelyn*, ii, p.166.

12 P. HUNNEYBALL, 'Cromwellian Style: The Architectural Trappings of the Protectorate Regime', in P. LITTLE (ed.), *The Cromwellian Protectorate* (Woodbridge, 2007), p.64.

13 The most thorough examination of the Protectoral Court remains, R. SHERWOOD, *The Court of Oliver Cromwell* (Totowa, 1977).

14 *Mercurius Politicus*, 369, pp.7882–4 (26 June 1657).

15 Brit. Lib., Lansdowne MS 95, fo. 37v.

16 HEATH, p.174.

17 *CSP Venetian 1657–9* (15/25 May 1657).

18 Bod. Lib. Tanner MS 51, fo. 1 (Letter to John Hobart, 12 Feb. 1658).

19 *Clarke Papers*, iii, p.127 (17 Nov. 1657).

20 *Ludlow*, i, p.185.

21 CARLYLE, iii, p.119.

22 *Ibid.*, i, pp.452–3.

23 *Ibid.*, ii, p.53.

24 NICKOLLS, *Original Letters*, p.40.

25 *Ibid.*, pp.6–7. (Thomas Patient to Oliver Cromwell).

26 *Thurloe SP*, vii, pp.492–3 (Henry to Richard Cromwell, 3 Nov. 1658).

27 CARLYLE, i, pp.292–3.

28 *Ibid.*, i, p.418.

29 *Ibid.*, i, p.451.

30 *Ibid.*, i, pp.452–3.

31 *Second Narrative of the Late Parliament, So Called* (London, 1658), p.13.

32 CARLYLE, ii, pp.422–3.

33 *Ibid.*, iii,190 (4 Feb. 1658).

34 *Thurloe SP*, vii, pp.363–4 (Thurloe to Henry Cromwell, 30 Aug. 1658).

35 *Ibid.*, vii, pp.372–3 (4 Sept. 1658).

36 *Ibid.*, vii, p.366.

37 TNA, PRO 31/17/33, p.1.

38 *Mercurius Politicus*, 434, pp.843–7 (18 Sept. 1658).

39 The problem of Richard's succession is discussed further in J. FITZGIBBONS, '"Not in any doubtfull dispute?", Reassessing the nomination of Richard Cromwell', *Historical Research* (forthcoming).

Chapter V

1 See Chapter IV for examples of Heath's work.

2 The 'tree' could be a reference to the Triple Tree at Tyburn.

3 J. CRANCH, *Narrative Relating to the Real Embalmed Head of Oliver Cromwell* (London, 1799), p.13.

4 For more discussion of Nonconformity and Cromwell see, BLAIR WORDEN, *Roundhead Reputations* (London, 2002), pp.250–59.

5 CARLYLE, ii, pp.293–4.

6 *Ibid.*, ii, pp.382–3.

7 *Ibid.*, ii, pp.535–6.

8 *Ibid.*, iii, pp.174–5 (25 Jan. 1658).

9 This conversion was not total, however. He refused to give his assent to an Act

of Parliament that would have brought back the practice of Catechising, for instance.

10 ABBOTT, iv, p.52.

11 *Ibid.*, iv, pp.52–3.

12 *Burton's Diary*, ii, pp.24–5.

13 *Ibid.*, ii, pp.25–6.

14 *Ibid.*, ii, p.49.

15 *Ibid.*, ii, p.78.

16 *Ibid.*, ii, pp.158, 166–7.

17 Quoted in WORDEN, *Roundhead Reputations*, p.247.

18 J.C. DAVIS, *Oliver Cromwell* (London, 2005), p.57.

19 WHITELOCKE, *Memoirals*, iii, p.5. (20 Apr. 1653).

20 *Ludlow*, i, p.353.

21 WHITELOCKE, *Memorials*, iii, p.6.

22 CARLYLE, ii, p.108.

23 *Ibid.*, ii, pp.282–3.

24 *Ibid.*, iii, p.101.

25 *Ibid.*, iii, p.189.

26 See Chapter 11.

27 See Chapter VI.

28 *Pittsburg Leader*, 24 October 1895. See Chapter 11.

Chapter VI

1 CARLYLE, i, pp.469–70.

2 G.K. CHESTERTON, *A Short History of England* (Toronto, 1917), p.134.

3 See Introduction.

Further Reading

Printed Editions of Primary Material

W.C. ABBOTT, *The Writings and Speeches of Oliver Cromwell* (4 vols, OUP reprint, 1989).

E.S. BEER (ed.), *The Diary of John Evelyn* (6 vols, OUP, 1955).

T. BIRCH (ed.), *A Collection of the State Papers of John Thurloe* (7 vols, London, 1742).

T. CARLYLE, *The Letters and Speeches of Oliver Cromwell*, ed. S.C. LOMAS (3 vols, Methuen & Co., 1904).

C.H. FIRTH (ed.), *Memoirs of Edmund Ludlow* (2 vols, Clarendon Press, 1894).

C.H. FIRTH (ed.), *The Clarke Papers* (4 vols, Camden Society, 1891–1901).

S.R. GARDINER (ed.), *The Constitutional Documents of the Puritan Revolution, 1625–60*, (3rd edn, Clarendon Press, 1906).

J. NICKOLLS (ed.), *Original Letters and Papers of State …* addressed to Oliver Cromwell (London, 1743).

N. PENNY (ed.), *The Journal of George Fox* (Dent, 1924).

J.T. RUTT (ed.), *The Diary of Thomas Burton Esq.*, (4 vols, Henry Colburn, London, 1828).

W.L. SACHSE (ed.), *The Diurnal of Thomas Rugge, 1659–1661* (Camden Society, 1961).

Secondary Material

M. BRIGHT and H.B. WHEATLEY (eds.), *The Diary of Samuel Pepys* (10 vols., George Bell & Sons, 1893–99)

B. COWARD, *Oliver Cromwell* (Longman, 1991).

B. COWARD, *The Cromwellian Protectorate* (Manchester University, 2002).

J.C. DAVIS, *Oliver Cromwell* (Arnold, 2005).

A. FRASER, *Cromwell Our Chief of Men* (Phoenix, 2002).

S.R. GARDINER, *History of the*

Great Civil War (4 vols, Phoenix, 2002).

P. GAUNT, *Oliver Cromwell* (Blackwell, 1997).

M. GUIZOT, *History of Richard Cromwell and the Restoration of Charles II*, A. Scoble, trans. (2 vols, Richard Bentley, 1856).

C. HOLMES, *Why Was Charles I Executed?* (Hambledon Continuum, 2006).

P. HUNNEYBALL, 'Cromwellian Style: The Architectural Trappings of the Protectorate Regime', in P. LITTLE (ed.), *The Cromwellian Protectorate* (Boydell, 2007).

L.L. KNOPPERS, *Constructing Cromwell: Ceremony, Portrait, and Print, 1645–1661* (CUP, 2000).

H.F. MCMAINS, *The Death of Oliver Cromwell* (Kentucky University, 2000).

J. MORRILL, 'The Making of Oliver Cromwell' in MORRILL (ed.), *Oliver Cromwell and the English Revolution* (Longman, 1990).

J. MORRILL, 'Rewriting Cromwell: A Case of Deafening Silences', *Canadian Journal of History* (2003).

M. NOBLE, *Memoirs of the Protectoral House of Cromwell*, (2 vols., London, 1787).

C. PARISH 'The posthumous history of Oliver Cromwell's head', in D. BEALES & H. NISBET (eds), *Sidney Sussex College Cambridge: Historical Essays in Commemoration of the Quatercentenary* (Boydell Press, 1996).

K. PEARSON and G. MORANT, 'The Wilkinson Head of Oliver Cromwell and Its Relationship to Busts, Masks and Painted Portraits', *Biometrika*, 26 (1934).

R. SHERWOOD, *The Court of Oliver Cromwell* (Rowman and Littlefield, 1977).

R. SHERWOOD, *Oliver Cromwell, King In All But Name* (Sutton, 1997).

F.J. VARLEY, *Oliver Cromwell's Latter End* (Chapman & Hall, 1939).

C.V. WEDGWOOD, *The Trial of Charles I* (Penguin, 2001).

A. WOOLRYCH, *Soldiers and Statesmen: The General Council of the Army and its Debate 1647–1648* (Clarendon Press, 1987).

B. WORDEN, *Roundhead Reputations: The English Civil Wars and the Passions of Posterity* (Penguin, 2002).

Index

Picture Credits

The publishers would like to thank the following for permission to reproduce their material. Every care has been taken to trace copyright holders, but we will be happy to rectify any omissions in future editions.

Acknowledgements

LIKE CROMWELL'S HEAD, this book has been an extraordinary journey shared by many people along the way. First of all, many thanks must go to the helpful staff of Sidney Sussex College, Cambridge— especially the archivist Nicholas Rogers and librarian Stewart Tiley. Equally praiseworthy was the assistance provided by the Cromwell Association in general, and John Goldsmith, curator of the Cromwell Museum, Huntingdon in particular. Sincere thanks are also due to Gillian Hawkins, who first suggested the idea of this book, and to Charlotte Rogers for her photography. I am also extremely grateful to Catherine Bradley, Slaney Begley, Ken Wilson, Tom Wharton and all the staff at the National Archives who have helped me through the various stages of the book's production. It has been both an invaluable opportunity and an unforgettable experience.

This book would not have been possible, however, if it were not for the continued support and advice of my colleagues and friends. There-fore, I wish to pay especial thanks to Paul Howard, Clive Holmes, George Southcombe and Daniel Walters for tirelessly commenting on numerous drafts and ideas relating to this work. Finally, I would like to thank my family for the unconditional encouragement they have given me both during this project and all the other times besides that—it is to them that I dedicate this book.